Jim Maynard's

POCKET
ASTROLOGER®
2001

Y0-BEO-847

The cover art for the 2001 Celestial Calendars is from an oil painting by Rodney Birkett. It was originally painted for the 1982 calendars, but not used until 1984. Rodney also painted the cover and zodiac illustrations for the 1991 calendars.

This year's zodiac illustrations were purchased from a European card manufacturer. Little information is available about the artist since the card company lost touch with her many years ago.

Pocket Astrologer® is also available as a 40-page wall calendar, the **Celestial Influences**®, which unfolds to 12 x 18 inches, has color illustrations and costs $9.95. A third format, **Celestial Guide**®, is a week-at-a-glance engagement calendar, 5½ x 8½ inches, 176 pages, illustrated, and has an ephemeris and address book. The **Celestial Guide**® is available in either a wire-O binding, $9.95, or as 3-hole punched, loose pages for your binder, also $9.95. See page 64 for ordering information.

Printed in Korea

Published by QUICKSILVER PRODUCTIONS
P. O. Box 340, Ashland, Oregon 97520 U.S.A.

Planetary Motions

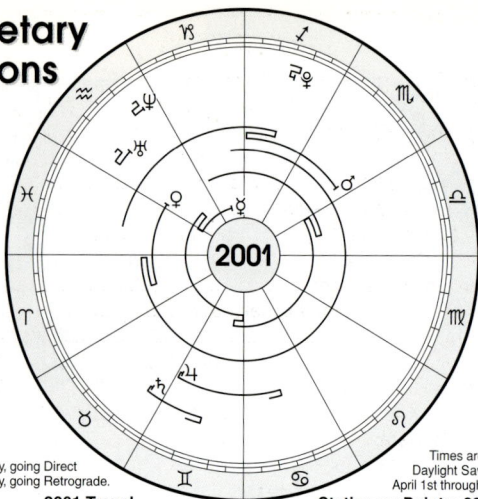

2001

SD = Stationary, going Direct
SR = Stationary, going Retrograde.

Times are corrected for
Daylight Saving Time from
April 1st through October 28th.

Planet	2001 Travel Begins	Ends	Date	Stationary Points: 2001 Pacific	Eastern	Position
Mercury ☿	15♑05	26♑21	SR February 3	5:58p	8:58p	0♓42
			SD February 25	7:41a	10:41a	15♒25
			SR June 3/4	10:22p	1:22a	29♊58
			SD June 27/28	10:49p	1:49a	21♊16
			SR October 1	12:23p	3:23p	29♎41
			SD October 22	5:23p	8:23p	14♎12
Venus ♀	27♒31	7♑47	SR March 8	5:07p	8:07p	17♈44
			SD April 19/20	9:34p	0:34a	1♈27
Mars ♂	5♏14	17♓15	SR May 11	9:08a	12:08p	29♐03
			SD July 19	3:45p	6:45p	15♐06
Jupiter ♃	2♊09℞	10♋36℞	SD January 25	0:38a	3:38a	1♊11
			SR November 2	7:35a	10:35a	15♋41
Saturn ♄	24♉04℞	9♊18℞	SD January 24	4:24p	7:24p	24♉04
			SR September 26	5:04p	8:04p	14♊58
Uranus ♅	18♒40	22♒29	SR May 29	8:11a	11:11a	24♒50
			SD October 30	2:55p	5:55p	20♒54
Neptune ♆	5♒21	7♒28	SR May 10	6:13p	9:13p	8♒47
			SD October 17	6:49p	9:49p	6♒00
Pluto ♇	13♐47	16♐03	SR March 17	6:36p	9:36p	15♐17
			SD August 23	9:06a	12:06p	12♐32

CONTENTS

Planets in Morning or Evening Twilight

	Morning	Evening
Mercury ☿	Feb. 19–April 15 June 26–July 29 Oct. 21–Nov. 18	Jan. 10–Feb. 7 May 1–June 7 Aug. 15–Oct. 8 Dec. 21–Dec. 31
Venus ♀	April 4–Dec. 3	Jan. 1–March 26
Mars ♂	Jan. 1–June 13	June 13–Dec. 31
Jupiter ♃	June 29–Dec. 31	Jan. 1–May 31
Saturn ♄	June 13–Dec. 3	Jan. 1–May 7 Dec. 3–Dec. 31

Signs of the Zodiac

♈ **Aries**, the first sign of the zodiac, is the emergence of the sprouting seed, the point of all beginnings. Aries is the outrushing force, sound and fury, primitive self-expression, the joy of being. Its forcefulness is like the ram which lowers its head and blindly charges. The Aries influence gives an adventurous, pioneering spirit, courage and a blunt and direct manner. The forcefulness of Aries is so strong that restrictions cannot be endured. Aries people are forever moving to new projects, seldom completing the old ones. An Aries person inhibited by daily routine and a sedentary life is likely to eventually explode. The "me first" attitude of Aries can go to the extremes of selfishness, crudeness, egotistical attitudes and foolhardiness if it's not tempered by sensitivity to others and strong guiding ideals.

♉ **Taurus** combines the concentrated nature of a fixed sign with the practicality of earth. Taurus people, being ruled by Venus, love beauty and are often quite charming. They're very affectionate, but their strong need for security sometimes lets their affectionate nature become possessive. Taurus people are strongly rooted in their opinions and can be stubborn and don't like to be contradicted. They *can* change but don't expect it to happen more than once! They're particularly patient and often reliable and practical, if their laziness and inertia don't get the better of them. Taurus people have incredible endurance and often have an excellent business sense. They crave luxury, art and good food.

♊ **Gemini** is a mutable air sign. Some people think Gemini has neither positive nor negative polarity. This is the sign of the twins, Castor and Pollux, who are the two sides of one personality. In Gemini the restless intelligence of air combines with the adaptability of a mutable sign. Ruled by Mercury, Gemini emphasizes communication. Geminis are versatile, logical, sometimes witty, inquisitive and spontaneous. They also tend to be nervous, restless, superficial and inconsistent. The metal of Gemini is Mercury which has no shape of its own. Try to hold it! It flows through your fingers as does the elusive Gemini.

♋ **Cancer**, with the unstable, emotional nature of water expressed in the cardinal mode, becomes restless. However, the self-repressive nature tends to keep this energy below the surface, with Cancers pursuing rather definite goals in secretive or unconscious ways. Much like their symbol the crab, Cancers can appear hard and insensitive on the outside, yet they are

4

soft and vulnerable on the inside, at times even overly sensitive and easily hurt. Like the crab, Cancers are evasive, always side-stepping, preferring not to confront anything too directly. They tend to hide within their shells and will often resist your prying into their secret lives.

Cancer is ruled by the Moon, giving it a flowing, emotional nature and an abundantly fertile imagination. Cancers are sensitive, cautious, kind, sympathetic, protective, shrewd and resourceful. However, their moody emotionalism can, at times, get out of hand.

♌ **Leo** combines the burning enthusiasm of fire with the powerful expression of its fixed nature. Leo is ruled by the strongest "planet," the Sun. Leos need to be the center of attention. They're creative, graceful, proud, dignified, determined and dramatic. They are very generous, enthusiastic, expansive and often good organizers. Their negative traits include being conceited, snobbish, intolerant, patronizing, dogmatic and pompous. Leos need to feel the divine nobility of their existence. Then they can allow their warm-heartedness to shine through and they can be tremendous sources of love and encouragement for others.

♍ **Virgo** is a practical earth sign, introverted like Taurus by its negative polarity, but enjoying the freedom and adaptability of its mutable nature. Virgo is addicted to practical, material objects but is not as possessive as Taurus. Virgo, like Gemini, is ruled by Mercury but here the communicative nature of Mercury is used on a practical level. Virgos are discriminating, critical, analytical, meticulous, modest and orderly. They can be worriers, overly fastidious, finicky, too critical and too conventional. Virgo's intellect lacks breadth, but it's great at details and facts. They analyze everything which is valuable in dealing with our bureaucratic modern society. Virgo desperately needs to work, to feel useful and to be of service to others.

♎ **Libra** is active and aggressive but not usually obviously. This mode of expression combines with the flowing communicative and intelligent nature of air signs. Libra's energy is searching for balance. While Libra is considered to have a positive polarity (yang), it is ruled by negative (yin) Venus, the receptive planet of charm and beauty. Libras idolize harmony. Sometimes, fearful of discord, they become indecisive. They easily see the value of each point of view, often because they don't hold a definite opinion of their own. In their search for balance, Libras strive to show both sides. Libras can be frivolous, gullible and flirtatious, but also diplomatic, idealistic, romantic, easygoing, and they have a refined appearance.

♏ **Scorpio**, a fixed sign, is true to its convictions, set in its ways. It's ruled by energetic Mars and by Pluto, the planet of intense desires. The negative polarity gives Scorpio a responsive nature, with much of its Martian forcefulness hidden from view. It's also a water sign, giving it an unstable, emotional nature with powerful feelings, emotions and a strong sense of purpose. The dichotomy of its fixity and instability often leaves Scorpio at war with itself. Scorpios are very imaginative, subtle, and determined, but can also be resentful, stubborn, secretive, suspicious and jealous. They're self-contained, may be self-centered, and have lots of stored energy ready to burst forth. Whatever Scorpios really want to achieve, they probably will. They have a great deal of personal magnetism and healing power.

♐ **Sagittarius** is the centaur shooting for great heights. Aspiration is their key. They aim high and they cover a lot of ground, even more than Gemini, their complement. They have the adaptability of a mutable sign, self-expressiveness of positive polarity, and the energy and enthusiasm of fire. Ruled by expansive Jupiter, they are travelers and philosophers. Sagittarians are freedom loving and need space. They're friendly, sincere, outgoing, versatile, dependable, open-minded, excitable, jovial, optimistic and can also be irresponsible, tactless, capricious, arrogant and dogmatic. But they can also be beautifully positive, encouraging people.

♑ **Capricorn**'s earthy, outgoing cardinality is applied on the practical level of everyday necessities. The sign's negative polarity gives Capricorns the ability to withdraw from the turbulence of the mainstream and to bide their time until the situation is ripe for their ambitions.

Capricorns are reliable, practical, ambitious, prudent, efficient, persistent and patient, and they have a good but dry sense of humor. Ruled by the contracting, concentrated energy of Saturn, they can also be cold and rigid, pessimistic and intolerably conventional. Saturn rulership also makes time important in Capricorn's life. They're often slow to develop, requiring more time than others. At middle age they often seem to be at a plateau, unchanging for decades, while their contemporaries age at a normal pace.

♒ **Aquarius**' outgoing, self-expressive positive polarity combines with the communicative nature of air. Intellectual Aquarians are disseminators of knowledge. With a fixed nature, they're unlikely to budge from their pre-conceived ideas but usually have a progressive outlook. They're original, inventive, friendly, independent, idealistic and revolutionary, sometimes even straining to be unconventional. They're very loving, but this is more easily expressed in a detached concern for groups rather than individuals. Aquarians, ruled by Uranus, the erratic revolutionary, must have their freedom and close personal relationships are often too restrictive.

♓ **Pisces** is unstable, flowing water combining with the mutable ability to easily drift through change making it the most fluid sign of the zodiac. The introverted nature of the negative polarity predominates. Pisces is the most sensitive of the signs with very strong and deep emotions. Pisceans are much too impressionable, too susceptible to outside influences and often need to escape. Ruled by the nebulous planet Neptune, they can be quite difficult to understand. It helps to remember that unworldly Pisceans operate on an intuitive level, often needing to retreat to maintain their equilibrium. They cannot be understood through logic, analysis or pressure. They can give vast amounts of compassion, are self-sacrificing, often kind, sympathetic, receptive, intuitive and humble. However, they can also be indecisive, vague, secretive, careless, and not good at dealing with the physical world.

the Planets

Planets are the focal points of energy. They're indicators of specific, unique kinds of activity, but colored by the nature of the sign the planet is in. The sign most like the nature of a particular planet is said to be ruled by that planet. Positive (yang) planets are the Sun, Mars, Jupiter, Uranus and Pluto. They activate, project, stimulate and vitalize. Negative (yin) planets, the Moon, Venus, Saturn and Neptune, are receptive, reactive, responsive and protective. Mercury is a neutral planet which modifies, interprets or communicates the energies of other planets in aspect to it.

☉ The **Sun** represents the will: the power urge, the vitalizing, life-giving force. It is the symbol of masculinity, paternity, authority, creative ability, ambition, pride, leadership, self-expression, determination and confidence. The Sun creates, achieves, elevates, dominates, sustains, fortifies, promotes and illuminates. It is the ruling planet of Leo, a sign of creativity and leadership. It is exalted in willful Aries indicating that the Sun's individuality can be expressed in a powerful and pure form through Aries.

☽ The **Moon** rules all things of a watery nature. It rules the tides and rhythms of the body as well as the oceans.

The Moon represents the personality, the subconscious or subjective mind and our instinctual behavior. It is associated with instincts, habits, memory, imagination, receptivity, impressionability, the desire for fresh experiences, femininity, maternity, fertility, disposition, emotions, feelings, moods, sensitivity, intuition, sensation and sympathy. The Moon is strongest in the nurturing sign of Cancer and weakest in the unreceptive, unemotional Capricorn. The Moon is also powerful in Taurus and emotionally problematic in Scorpio.

☿ **Mercury** represents the mind—the link between spirit and matter, between soul and personality. Mercury symbolizes the power of communication and interpretation: intelligence, reasoning capacities and the ability to perceive relationships and gather facts. Mercurial qualities also include being adaptable, attentive, perceptive, clever, versatile, inconsistent, hypercritical, argumentative, sarcastic, cynical, excitable, impressionable, and nervous or prone to worry. Mercury narrates, talks, memorizes, debates, writes, argues, analyzes, studies, travels, sells, reflects and expresses with the hands as well as the tongue.

Mercury is of neither positive nor negative polarity—neither masculine nor feminine. Mercury rules all communications and is associated with speaking and writing, educational capacities and manual skills.

Mercury is especially active in the versatile, talkative sign of Gemini, and its nature is stronger in analytical Virgo. Pure Mercurial expression becomes difficult in Sagittarius and in Pisces, which relate and communicate more through hopes and beliefs than through facts.

♀ **Venus**, the Roman goddess of beauty, is associated with the power of love, the power of attraction and cohesion and the power of quiet, gentle persuasion. It stimulates the desire to be sociable. Its influences include balancing, harmonizing and peacemaking. It is symbolic of affection, sentiment, sympathy, romance, friendship, beauty, pleasure, music, manners, art, attractiveness, values, appreciation and a sense of aesthetics.

If afflicted (adversely aspected to other planets), the affectionate, warm and sympathetic nature of Venus can be flirtatious, self-indulgent, sensual, vain, lazy and irresponsible.

Venus rules placid Taurus as well as Libra, the sign of harmony. A strong Venus influence has a mellowing effect. The Venus nature is more than gentle—it is graceful and tactful. Venus is not easily expressed in the intense signs of Scorpio or Aries. Virgo, because of its excessive criticism and fussiness, can also inhibit the expression of Venus, whereas the loving nature of Pisces reinforces the Venusian influence.

♂ **Mars** is the complement of Venus. Mars is yang, positive, outgoing energy, masculine in nature. It is a planet of desire, energy and action. As the ancient god of war, Mars represents struggles within and with others. It is closely related to our physical energy, and it rules our animal essence. Martian expressions include desire, courage, initiative, executive ability, assertiveness, aggressiveness, impulsiveness, adventurousness, self-will, resistance, rashness (leading to accidents) and aggressive sexual love.

Mars rules forceful Aries and determined Scorpio. The aggressive nature of Mars is also easily expressed in the ambitious sign of Capricorn. The driving force of Mars is restrained when it falls in the partnership sign, Libra, or the easygoing Taurus. The receptive nature of Cancer is also not compatible with the assertiveness of Mars.

♃ **Jupiter** is larger than all the other planets combined. It is symbolic of expansion, the higher mind, wisdom, enthusiasm, optimism, spontaneity, benevolence, generosity, the desire to gain through experience, and the urge to improve the state of things. Jupiter represents increase, opportunity, rewards, abundance, tolerance, charity, philanthropy, ethics, faith, confidence, idealism, aspiration, justice, loyalty, self-indulgence, joviality, extravagance and conceit. Jupiter protects, assists, magnifies, inflates, gives, speculates, inspires, encourages, counsels and philosophizes. It carries the ability to grow in physical, mental and moral directions.

Jupiter is most at home in Sagittarius where the desire for a variety of experiences can bring wisdom. Expansive Jupiter is limited by the trivial mental nature of Gemini. Virgo can impede Jupiter with its preoccupation for detail. Free-flowing, imaginative Pisces reinforces Jupiter.

♄ **Saturn** symbolizes the first law of manifestation—limitation. Saturn strengthens the personality through endurance and persistence. It focuses and concentrates energy. Saturn's contractive nature gives us the opportunity for introspection, meditation and concentration—to work out karma in the process of evolution. The key to dealing with Saturn is discipline. Saturn requires caution, restraint, seriousness and stability. It is also related to time, organization, consolidation, self-preservation, crystallization, ambition, responsibility, conventionality, pessimism and perseverance. Saturn inhibits, delays, restricts, perfects and deepens. It causes fear, worry and anxiety.

Saturn is most compatible with Capricorn, the sign of material organization and practical ambition. Saturn is ill-expressed in Cancer where it becomes hypersensitive. Saturn exalts in the balancing act of Libra and finds the impulsive nature of Aries at odds with its cautious approach.

♅ **Uranus** has a nature similar to Mercury in its nervous and mental impact, but it is much more powerful, violent, fanatical and harder to handle for the physical body. Uranus represents the freedom urge. It is the planet of extremes and sudden change. It's a force which destroys the old to allow room for the new. Uranus destroys the constricting influence and crystallizations of Saturn. It displaces and overthrows the established attitudes which have outlived their usefulness. The old must be destroyed before the new can come, but we are often fearful of new, unknown ways and reluctant to let go. Uranus makes us let go. It shakes us loose!

The nature of Uranus has an exciting, uprooting and awakening effect. It brings disruption, anarchy, rebellion, revolution, freedom, individualism, altruism, originality, invention, experimentation, instability, erratic action and detachment. It is related to intuitive knowledge.

♆ **Neptune** is often considered a higher vibration of Venus. It symbolizes receptivity, passivity, impressionability and nebulousness. Neptune brings either spiritual strength or escapist tendencies—seeking the path of least resistance. Neptune can offer spiritual guidance and protection, or entice us to avoid all responsibility. Other Neptunian traits include being idealistic, imaginative, intuitive, subtle, artistically creative, evasive, deceitful (to yourself as well as to others), hypersensitive, careless, sentimental, scattered, indecisive, impractical and compassionate. Neptune is the god of oceans. It rules the watery sign of Pisces and is inhibited in the earthy, orderly, practical and constricting sign of Virgo, the opposite of Pisces. Neptune expresses its nature well through inspirational Sagittarius. It is inhibited by the mundane level of the daily affairs of Gemini.

♇ **Pluto** can be considered the higher octave of Mars. Pluto represents those elements which have not yet been integrated into the collective consciousness. Pluto represents the urge to transform and to regenerate bringing rebirth. It is a symbol of decay, contamination, infection, destruction, desire, obsessions, disintegration and elimination, but also a symbol of a cleansing, healing catharsis.

Aspects

Planets form various angular relationships to each other which are called aspects. Imagine an aspect as the blending rays of two planets.

✳ The **sextile**, 60°, is a favorable aspect, the planets usually being in congenial signs of compatible elements. This aspect can allow the influences of the planets to work in harmony. However, the sextile only brings opportunity. These opportunities must be acted upon to be of use.

☐ The **square**, 90°, is regarded as unfavorable. It represents the struggle of two forces at cross-purposes. The square brings stress and denotes obstacles which can inspire growth through concentrated effort.

△ The **trine**, 120°, the most harmonious aspect, usually joins planets in congenial signs of the same element. Energies combine with ease. The drawback is the lack of challenge–getting benefits without effort.

☍ The **opposition**, 180° (☽= Lunar Eclipse), when planets are exactly opposite each other, causes stress and awareness. This polarity, though tense, does not have to be discordant as opposites are complementary.

☌ The **conjunction** (☉ = Solar Eclipse or Lunar occultation), is when two planets are at the same degree of longitude (or within orb). It gives great strength to the energies of the interacting planets and can be either harmonious or discordant depending upon the nature of the planets involved. More can be determined about the nature of a particular conjunction by comparing the nature of the sign in which it occurs to the natures of the planets involved. A planet strongly compatible to the sign of conjunction can dominate the energies of the other planet.

Orbs: Aspects given in the calendar are listed at their exact times. This is when they are strongest but the influences are present before and after the aspect is exact. This aura of influence is called the orb.

Delineation: Consider the meaning of the aspect, the natures and combined meanings of the planets, and the strength of the planets by virtue of their signs.

☽☌☿ **Moon conjunct Mercury:** Intellect and feelings are working together. Mentality is active, alert and sensitive. Nervous systems are highly tuned and very responsive. People are talkative and intellectually attuned to intuitions and emotions.

☽⚹☿, ☽△☿ **Moon sextile** or **trine Mercury:** Communication and conversation are easy with this positive connection of mind and emotions. Practical mental abilities and good common sense mentality are highlighted. It is a good time to conduct business which utilizes communications media or to engage in writing of any sort.

☽□☿, ☽☌☿ **Moon square** or **opposite Mercury:** Minds are acute but restless and excitable. Nervous systems function poorly. The unconscious mind will interfere with the conscious reasoning process. Preoccupation with the past can interfere with one's objectivity and open-mindedness. Concern with trivialities and emotional whims might block meaningful mental pursuits. Incessant talking can drain everyone's energy. This is a very poor time for communications with the public. Nervous energy can cause digestive difficulties.

☽☌♀ **Moon conjunct Venus:** There is a good balanced outlook on life and a love of beauty. The emotional response to beauty and harmony heightens artistic abilities. Sensitivity and affections are strong as subconscious sensuality seeks emotional satisfaction. This is a good time for romance or for any social gathering. Have a party!

☽⚹♀, ☽△♀ **Moon sextile** or **trine Venus:** Generally similar to the conjunction, but more pronounced. Personalities mellow. Dispositions are pleasant. There is an increased interest in the arts.

☽□♀, ☽☌♀ **Moon square** or **opposite Venus:** There is an inability to express emotions and affections. There might be unhappiness and disappointments in emotional relationships. People become moody and overly sensitive. There are material and domestic difficulties. This is not recommended as a time for organizing social events.

☽☌♂ **Moon conjunct Mars:** Brings moodiness, aggressiveness, impulsive actions. Feelings are strong and outbursts of anger are likely. People seem opinionated and are also likely to feel courageous.

☽⚹♂, ☽△♂ **Moon sextile** or **trine Mars:** This brings good emotional and physical health, a lot of energy and emotional force. There are opportunities for material enterprises or for home improvements.

☽□♂, ☽☌♂ **Moon square** or **opposite Mars:** A time of delicate health and strong, volatile emotions. It is easy to be quarrelsome, get upset and lose tempers. People are irritable, impulsive and self-indulgent.

☽☌♃ **Moon conjunct Jupiter:** People are sympathetic and generous. There is concern with the social welfare. This conjunction brings good health and optimism along with a possible urge for change.

☽⚹♃, ☽△♃ **Moon sextile** or **trine Jupiter:** Brings pleasant temperaments and kind dispositions. Domestic peace and happiness become important. It is a good time for business.

☽□♃, ☽☍♃ **Moon square** or **opposite Jupiter:** Financial judgment is not good. Tendencies are to extravagance, foolish generosity and laziness. Overeating is likely. Spiritual doubts may arise.

☽☌♄ **Moon conjunct Saturn:** Opportunity for hard work. Orderliness and duty become important. People are inclined to be critical and stingy, timid, cautious and possibly feeling inadequate. Depression is very possible.

☽⚹♄, ☽△♄ **Moon sextile** or **trine Saturn:** Benefits come through a willing acceptance of duty. There can be gains by keeping things practical and orderly. Physical comforts seem of little importance.

☽□♄, ☽☍♄ **Moon square** or **opposite Saturn:** There is a lack of emotional flexibility or optimism. Depression. Judgmental attitudes may block abilities to respond to others in an appropriate way. Life is just hard.

☽☌♅ **Moon conjunct Uranus:** Be ready for sudden changes of mood and impulsive, unexpected actions. High emotional tension and freedom-seeking urges arise.

☽⚹♅, ☽△♅ **Moon sextile** or **trine Uranus:** Ambition and intuition are strong. Feelings of independence and self-reliance surface. There is much energy in the air. This aspect gives rise to an inventive, original, spontaneous imagination. Psychic abilities can become highly tuned. Changeable moods help break through inhibiting patterns, bringing opportunities to evolve. New friends are often found.

☽□♅, ☽☍♅ **Moon square** or **opposite Uranus:** Disruptions. Obsessions with the unusual and unconventional. Independence is so important that communicative contact with others is difficult. People become restless, irritable and stubborn and might be prone to accidents.

☽☌♆ **Moon conjunct Neptune:** A time of warm kindness, sympathy and understanding. Emotions and psychic inclinations are strong and feelings are vulnerable. It is easy to drift into a dream world as Neptune makes people very impressionable. Check out the sign this aspect is in and how it relates to your natal chart.

☽⚹♆, ☽△♆ **Moon sextile** or **trine Neptune:** Sensitivity opens the unconsciousness. Imagination is strong and inspirational.

☽□♆, ☽☍♆ **Moon square** or **opposite Neptune:** Self-deception is easy. Difficult emotional relationships and strong escapist tendencies arise.

☽☌♀ **Moon conjunct Pluto:** Moods and impulsiveness may lead to new emotional foundations.

☽⚹♀, ☽△♀ **Moon sextile** or **trine Pluto:** Strong emotional outbursts may become disruptive but for the better.

☽□♀, ☽☍♀ **Moon square** or **opposite Pluto:** Emotions are stifled. People are uneasy. Jealousy is likely. Secrets are revealed.

☽☌☉ **Moon conjunct Sun (New Moon):** Harmony, vitality, and determination increase as well as inclinations to instinctual activity.

☽⚹☉, ☽△☉ **Moon sextile** or **trine Sun:** Feelings and thinking can be easily aligned. Inner conflicts float away. Ambition ebbs as the feeling of contentment rides high. Harmony is everywhere. People can "let it be."

☽□☉ **Moon square Sun (First or Last Quarter):** Tensions and conflicts erupt between desires and emotions as people struggle for fulfillment.

☽☍☉ **Moon opposite Sun (Full Moon):** Emotions, self-confidence and energy can go to extreme highs or lows as people crest on the waves of the preceding New Moon and the perspectives that have or haven't developed through the first two lunar phases.

Moon through the Signs

☽ in ♈ When the Moon passes through **Aries**, ruled by Mars, people are highly enthusiastic. It is a period of ambition and energetic activity. It is a good time for beginning projects and instigating change. Be aware the desire for change will be based more upon impulse than reason. Watch for temperamental flare-ups and selfishness. With all this forceful energy, it is important to be mindful of the rights of others. Aries, which rules the head, is known for its headstrong behavior. While the Moon is in Aries people are susceptible to head injuries.

☽ in ♉ When the Moon goes into **Taurus**, the aggressive, charging Aries ram mellows into the solid, placid bull. Remember the term "bull-headed," as people will now tend to be very cautious and unchanging, leaning toward stubbornness. There is a feeling that it is necessary to protect the status quo or what one already has (key phrase is "I have"). The need for financial and material security is strong. While the Moon is in Taurus take time to continue or finish projects already started. Venus rules Taurus, so this would be a good time to enjoy and appreciate the earthly beauty which surrounds us. Taurus rules the throat.

☽ in ♊ While the Moon is in the dualistic sign of **Gemini**, we may never make up our minds. With the Gemini ease of seeing both sides of every-thing we feel more adaptable, changeable and talkative. Gemini being ruled by Mercury makes this a time for communication. It is a good time to write, take care of puzzling tasks, make speeches, or just let ideas soar through the clouds. Intellectual pursuits and mind games may become more prominent than practical concerns. People begin to feel restless and there is an inclination to rationalize emotions. A spontaneous tongue may hastily express things which are only true for the moment. Gemini rules the lungs, arms, hands and nervous system.

☽ in ♋ Since **Cancer** is ruled by the Moon, lunar influences are strongest and most easily expressed when focused through Cancer. The Moon greatly influences the personality, the subconscious and the emotions and molds instinctual behavior. When the Moon is in Cancer, it is a time of intense emotions and great sensitivity with people responding to life through emotions rather than reason. During this very vulnerable period be cautious not to emotionally wound others or allow yourself to be wounded. Generally, people will be passive, easy-going, sentimental, lov-ing and nurturing. This motherly expression of caring is often expressed with food and it is easy to overeat. Cancer rules the breasts and stomach. Cancer is a nurturing sign and the most fertile sign of the zodiac.

☽ in ♌ Under the influence of the Moon in **Leo**, people need romance, affection and recognition. The desire to be admired and appreciated can be so strong that it may result in especially dramatic behavior. Leo is ruled by the Sun making this a time of ambition, independence and leadership. People may refuse to recognize limitations. The Moon in Leo is a time of enjoyment and warmth and a time to show kindness and generosity to others. Leo rules the heart and the upper spine.

☽ in ♍ **Virgo**, like Gemini, is ruled by Mercury. While the Moon is in Virgo, it is also a good time for intellectual pursuits, but now it is better for those requiring critical detail rather than innovative creativity. This is a good time for taking care of any matter requiring painstaking attention. People may become shy and retiring with the Moon passing through Virgo and tend to be discriminating, fastidious and overly critical. These influences lead to concern about food and health for Virgo rules the intestines and the powers of assimilation. Many people feel the urge to clean up their homes at this time which is a good way to channel Virgo energy.

☽ in ♎ While the Moon is in **Libra** people have a strong sensitivity to and attraction for others. This comes from the Libran search for harmony and balance, for the Libra nature accentuates teamwork. It is a good time to form partnerships of all natures (friendships, marriage, business). Libra is ruled by Venus which manifests as a friendly and tolerant nature and a desire to beautify. It is an excellent time for artistic work as the beauty of Venus is combined with the intellectual ease of an air sign. It is a good time for a social gathering, when the consciousness of self, as expressed in the first six signs of the zodiac, becomes united with the awareness of the needs and desires of others. The Libra keynote is "I balance," as in yin/yang, day/night, me/you, summer/winter.

Libra rules the kidneys and lower back. Be careful not to imbibe too many impurities during this time when the kidneys are so vulnerable.

☽ in ♏ **Scorpio** is ruled by Mars and Pluto. Mars' influence brings out strong passions and Pluto shows very strong desires. People often get aggressive, critical, impatient and moody. There is a marked increase of intensity and a heightened sensitivity to personal offenses and insults. Remember that Scorpio has a suspicious and secretive nature. Avoid social complications. Beware of jealousy. Watch out for the Scorpion sting. Remember to forgive and forget. Be cautious interacting with the opposite sex; however, it could be a good time for an intense merging with another on a deep emotional level. Scorpio rules the generative system, organs of reproduction and the lower spine. The Moon in Scorpio is a very bad time for surgical operations.

☽ in ♐ The Moon in **Sagittarius** can give an idealistic feeling, or a sense of discontinuity, restlessness, desire for adventures and sports, a love of change and motion, and the itch to travel. People will be warm and friendly since Sagittarius is ruled by expansive Jupiter but may also have a strong need for independence and feel unable to endure restrictions. People will likely feel spontaneous, intuitive (prophetic) and animated with a tendency toward superficial enthusiasm. Here the Moon stimulates our aspirations for self-improvement and brings a philosophical influence. It is a good time for intellectual affairs, promoting ideas through publishing, lecturing, etc., or dealing with institutions of learning. Sagittarius rules the thighs and hips.

☽ in ♑ With the Moon in **Capricorn** the vibrations of Saturn are emphasized. This brings contraction following Jupiter's expansive influence in Sagittarius. It's a time of material ambition and work and duty. Spiritual and intellectual interests fall away. In the search for status and financial security, people might become insensitive, even unsympathetically cruel, but from selfish necessity rather than animosity.

The Saturn influence of Capricorn causes pessimism or negative outlooks to creep in. While the Moon is in Capricorn energy is generally sluggish. It is a time to diligently apply ourselves to tasks while living solely in the present. Capricorn rules the knees, teeth, bones and skin.

☽ in ♒ **Aquarius** is ruled by Uranus. While the Moon is in Aquarius, public affairs become more important as there is an increased interest in the welfare of others in a social sense. People are very friendly but in an impersonal manner. Uranus brings the desire for freedom and a love for the innovative and unconventional. People are now operating from intellectual rather than emotional motivations and will be searching for the freedom to express personal thoughts and uniqueness, and may be demanding the freedom to come and go without restrictions. Aquarius rules the ankles, the circulation, the electrical forces in the body and the nervous system.

☽ in ♓ **Pisces** is ruled by Neptune which brings an inclination toward psychic impressions. Imagination is strong and there is a heightened sensitivity to music and other intangible forces. There are tendencies to be emotional, spiritual, and self-sacrificing, plus a developing impressionability which can give a feeling of being too vulnerable, drifting into withdrawal for emotional protection. People may feel passive, sentimental, gentle, kind, and cheerful, but too easily discouraged. Some people experience stirrings of vague memories (often identified as past lives) or insights into the spiritual meaning of current situations. Pisces rules the feet.

the Lunar Cycle

From New Moon to Full Moon, the first two quarters, the Moon is increasing in light, or waxing. This period of increasing light is traditionally the time for new beginnings, new projects and ideas, for growth. The waxing Moon is a time of spontaneous and instinctual action.

Should your new ideas or projects come to an impasse, this might be broken at the Full Moon. The waning Moon, from one Full Moon to the next New Moon, is a time for conscious growth as the Moon dissipates its collected solar potential. The time of the waxing Moon is in many traditions concerned more with mundane outer matters, whereas the period of the waning Moon deals with subconscious enlightenment leading to the clarification of conscious values. The waxing Moon brings instinctual growth. The waning Moon brings a conscious process of creative release.

The New Moon (☽☌☉) begins a new cycle. It is the seed of the beginning lunar cycle. The chart of the New Moon is the key to influences in the coming lunar month.

The First Quarter (☽□☉) is the beginning of the second phase. Beginning with the seed of the New Moon, growth in consciousness might be impeded by obstacles from the past. Ideally, these will be overcome by the First Quarter, a point of focus which illustrates the necessity for change. This must happen if the energy released with the coming Full Moon is to be utilized. If rejection of the shackles from the past is incomplete and if growth is lethargic, then the illumination and growth offered during this cycle cannot be fully integrated. It may even sour. Whatever patterns are set at the First Quarter will continue to develop throughout the lunar cycle.

The Full Moon (☽☍☉) illuminates the seed and potential of the New Moon. The third quarter, Full Moon to Last Quarter, ideally brings clarification to the influences of the entire lunar cycle. If a positive attitude of growth has developed and if the restrictions of the past were thrown off during the waxing Moon, then the Full Moon can now bring fulfillment and a renewed sense of determination and resolve. However if a negative attitude has dominated the period of increasing light, then the Full Moon might bring serious mental, and possibly physical, conflicts.

The fourth quarter is from the Last Quarter (☽□☉) to the next New Moon. It can bring a crisis in consciousness. This cycle's experiences have culminated and one must now prepare for rebirth as the process repeats itself with the next New Moon.

Moon Void of Course

As the Moon orbits the Earth it passes through the signs of the zodiac. Every lunar month it travels through all twelve signs, passing through each in more than two, but less than three days. When the Moon gets near the end of each sign, it goes beyond its last major aspect, or connection, with another planet. When this happens, and until it moves into the next sign, the Moon is said to be "Void of Course." This period is a time when we can really feel unconnected and without direction. It is, therefore, an ideal time for centering ourselves.

The void of course condition may occur for only seconds or minutes of time or it may last for a day or two. It all depends on the locations of the planets and their interactions at the time.

While the Moon is void of course (V/c) it is wise to avoid making important decisions. Judgment at this time is probably faulty. Decisions tend to be unrealistic, subject to factors unknown at the time. New paths are likely to be plagued with false starts, errors and unexpected hassles.

During Moon void of course, actions produce unexpected results. Creative efforts go in unexpected directions. Contracts, promises or new laws bring on difficulties. Purchases prove to be unsatisfactory or the object simply does not fulfill its intention. Routines involving no decisions will usually go well but often require corrections later. Delays and frustrations are common. Moon void of course is a time to "kick back," let life flow and avoid difficulties.

Presidential candidates Dewey, Nixon (vs. Kennedy), Goldwater, and McGovern were all nominated while the Moon was void of course. Nixon was elected in 1972 while the Moon was void of course. The Watergate break-in occurred during a void of course Moon. And President Ford was sworn in with the Moon void of course.

The important guideline for Moon void of course periods is to not be involved in concerns beyond your spiritual center. Moon void of course is a time for subjective, spiritual, non-materialistic concerns. Don't push the river!

Once the Moon enters the next sign, if we have taken time off from business to give attention to relaxation and to our spiritual growth, then we can more effectively go back to dealing with the affairs of the day-to-day material world.

Planting by the Moon

The Moon governs growth. Planting is most productive if the lunar influences are considered. We have long heard sayings about planting by the light or dark of the Moon. These old sayings refer to the phases of the Moon, which are the angular relationships of the forces of the Sun and Moon. However, it is important to also consider the nature of the sign of the zodiac through which the Moon is passing.

For best results plant, graft or transplant annuals which bear above-ground crops during the Moon's first and second quarters. (An "annual" is a plant which completes the entire life cycle in one growing season.) During the first and second quarters, New Moon to Full Moon, the Moon is increasing in light. This is known as the waxing Moon.

Following the Full Moon are the third and the fourth quarters. This phase is the "dark of the Moon" or the waning Moon. The third quarter is the best time for pruning, the planting of biennials, perennials and bulb and root crops. These can also be planted in the fourth quarter if necessary. However, the fourth quarter is best suited for tilling and destroying weeds and pests. It is also the best phase for cultivation and harvesting. Remember, the New Moon to the Full Moon is the time to make new beginnings, the time to increase. The Full Moon to the next New Moon is a time to bring affairs together or to a close.

The bruised areas of fruit picked in the first and second quarters will rot more easily whereas the bruised areas of fruit picked in the third and fourth quarters will dry. You can retard your lawn's growth by cutting the grass during the waning Moon. Conversely, you can stimulate its growth by cutting it during the waxing Moon. Timber will season better if it is cut in the fourth quarter in a barren sign.

The most fertile signs, the water signs Cancer, Scorpio and Pisces, are best for planting. The signs Capricorn, Taurus and Libra are the next best signs. Taurus and Capricorn will produce strong, hardy plants. For beautiful and fragrant flowers plant while the Moon is in Libra, which is ruled by Venus, the goddess and planet of beauty. The least productive times for planting are Aries, Gemini, Leo, Virgo, Sagittarius and Aquarius.

The first day the Moon is in a sign is better for planting than is the second. The second day is better than the third. The influence of each sign is greatly intensified when the Sun and Moon are in the same sign.

Time Corrections

Times given in this calendar are either **Pacific Standard Time** or **Pacific Daylight Saving Time.** Calculations given with each monthly calendar express Daylight Saving Time from the first Sunday in April through the last Sunday in October. If your locality is not using Daylight Saving Time, then subtract one hour from the times given for the summer months.

Pacific Time is corrected to **Rocky Mountain Time** by adding one hour. For **Central Time**, add two hours. For **Eastern Time**, add three hours. For **Alaskan Time**, subtract one hour. For **Hawaii-Aleutian Time**, subtract two hours. For **Greenwich Mean Time**, add eight hours to Pacific Standard Time or seven hours to Pacific Daylight Saving Time.

For other localities, use the Time Zone Map below. Count the number of zones your position is from Pacific Time (+8). Add (or subtract) one hour for each zone you are to the right (or left) of column "+8."

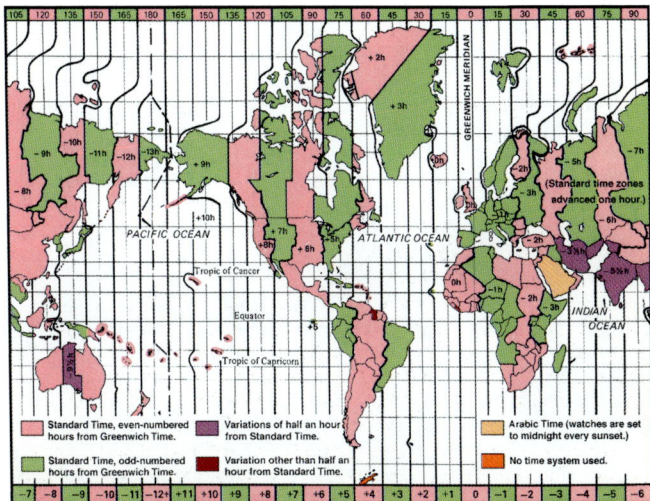

Standard Time, even-numbered hours from Greenwich Time.

Variations of half an hour from Standard Time.

Arabic Time (watches are set to midnight every sunset.)

Standard Time, odd-numbered hours from Greenwich Time.

Variation other than half an hour from Standard Time.

No time system used.

JANUARY 2001

Day	☉	☿	♀	♂	♃	♄	♅	♆	♇	☊
1	12♑	16♈	28≈	06♏	02 R	25 R	19≈	05≈	14 ♐	16♋
2	13	18	29	06	02♊	25	19	05	14	16
3	14	19	00♓	07	02	24	19	05	14	16
4	15	21	01	08	02	24	19	06	14	15
5	16	22	03	08	02	24	19	06	14	15
6	17	24	04	09	02	24	19	06	14	15
7	18	26	05	09	02	24	19	06	14	15
8	19	27	06	10	02	24	19	06	14	15
9	20	29	07	10	02	24	19	06	14	15
10	21	01≈	08	11	02	24	19	06	14	15
11	22	02	09	11	01	24	19	06	14	15
12	23	04	10	12	01	24	19	06	14	15
13	24	05	11	12	01	24	19	06	14	15
14	25	07	12	13	01	24	19	06	14	15
15	26	09	13	13	01	24	19	06	14	15
16	27	11	14	14	01	24	20	06	14	14
17	28	12	15	14	01	24	20	06	14	14
18	29	14	16	15	01	24	20	06	14	14
19	00≈	16	17	15	01 D	24	20	06	15	14
20	01≈	17	18	16	01	24 D	20	06	15	14
21	02	19	19	17	01	24	20	06	15	14
22	03	20	20	17	01	24	20	06	15	14
23	04	22	21	18	01	24	20	06	15	14
24	05	23	22	19	01	24	20	06	15	14
25	06	25	23	19	01	24	20	06	15	14
26	07	26	24	20	01	24	20	06	15	14
27	08	27	25	21	01	24	20	06	15	14
28	09	28	26	21	01	25	20	06	15	14
29	10	28	27	22	01	25	20	06	15	14
30	11	29	28	23	01	25	20	06	15	14
31	12	01≈	30	23	01	25	20	06	15	14

Above are rounded to nearest whole degree. Positions more than 29°30′round to 30° of one sign before 00′ of the next sign. See pages 46-57 for a complete ephemeris.

JANUARY PLANTING DAYS
Above-ground crops: Best days: 8, 9, 26, 27, 28 Good days: 4, 5, 31
Root crops & perennials: Best days: 16, 17, 18 Good: 14, 15, 21, 22, 23

PLANET VISIBLE IN THE MORNING SKY
Mars.

PLANETS VISIBLE IN THE EVENING SKY
Mercury from the 10th, Venus, Jupiter, and Saturn.

CAPRICORN ♑ December 21 to January 19 "I USE"
A cardinal, earth sign of negative polarity.
SYMBOL: the mountain goat with a dolphin's tail ascending the
heights from the depths of the sea. COLORS: dark shades.
RULING PLANET: Saturn. RULES the bones, skin, knees.
KEYWORDS: ambitious, conscientious, prudent, reliable, patient.

DECEMBER 2000 S M T W T F S 1 2 3 4 5 6 7 8 9 10 11 12 13 14 15 16 17 18 19 20 21 22 23 24 25 26 27 28 29 30 31 **FEBRUARY 2001** S M T W T F S 1 2 3 4 5 6 7 8 9 10 11 12 13 14 15 16 17 18 19 20 21 22 23 24 25 26 27 28	**1** ☽v/c 3:36a ☽→♈ 2:14p ☽⚹♄ 3:36a ♂□♆ 9:02a ☽⚹♃ 6:20p **New Year's Day** Grandmaster Flash 1958	**2** First Qtr. 12♈37 2:31p ☽ in ♈ ☽⚹♆ 0:40a ☽□☉ 2:31p ☽△♇ 4:51p Isaac Asimov 1920 Christy Turlington 1969	**3** ☽v/c 2:09a ☽→♉ 10:57p ☽□☿ 0:58a ☽⚹♅ 2:09a ♀→♓ 10:14a John Paul Jones 1946 Victoria Principal 1950	**4** ☽ in ♉ ☽⚹♀ 0:06a ☽□♆ 8:51a ☽☍♂ 11:55a Grace Bumbry 1937 Melissa Morgan 1964	**5** ☽ in ♉ ☽v/c 6:09p ☽△☉ 2:04a ♀□♃ 3:14a ☽□♅ 8:37a ☽△☿ 2:38p ☽☌♄ 6:09p Carl Evans 1968 Chris Stein 1950	**6** ☽→♊ 3:44a ☽☌♃ 6:45a ☽□♀ 9:10a ☽△♆ 1:04p ☿△♄ 7:46p Gustave Dore 1832 John Singleton 1966
7 ☽ in ♊ ☽v/c 11:19a ☽☍♇ 3:07a ☽△♅ 11:19a Erin Gray 1952 Nicholas Cage 1964	**8** ☽→♋ 5:09a ☽△♀ 2:05p ☽△♂ 8:38p Andre Ribeiro 1966 Shirley Bassey 1937	**9** **Lunar Eclipse** Full Moon 19♋39 12:24p ☽ in ♋ ☽☍☉ 12:24p ☽⚹♄ 7:41p Mark Martin 1959 Kimberly Beck 1956	**10** ☽v/c 4:39a ☽→♌ 4:44a ☽☍☿ 4:39a ☿→♒ 5:26a ☽⚹♃ 7:12a ☽☍♆ 1:42p ☽□♂ 9:55p Donald Fagen 1948 Krista Tesreau 1964	**11** ☽ in ♌ ☽v/c 7:08p ☽△♇ 3:03a ☿△♃ 3:21a ☽☍♅ 11:07a ☽□♄ 7:08p Mary J. Blige 1971 Ben Crenshaw 1952	**12** ☽→♍ 4:26a ☽□♃ 6:48a ☽☍♀ 8:51p Sport Spice 1974 Allan Dean Feuerbach 1948	**13** ☽ in ♍ ☽v/c 8:12p ☽⚹♂ 0:06a ☽□♇ 3:34a ☿☌♆ 5:10p ☽△☉ 8:00p ☽△♄ 8:12p ☉△♄ 10:49p Patrick Dempsey 1966 Brock(man) Adams 1927
14 ☽→♎ 6:05a ☽△♃ 8:27a ☽△♆ 4:07p ☽△☿ 7:09p Tom Tryon 1926 Yukio Mishima 1925	**15** ☽ in ♎ ☽⚹♇ 6:47a ☽△♅ 3:57p Ronnie Van Zant 1949 **Martin L. King, Jr. Day**	**16** Last Qtr. 26♎27 4:35a ☽v/c 4:35a ☽→♏ 11:02a ☽□☉ 4:35a ☽□♆ 9:56p ♀□♇ 10:35p ♀△♂ 11:58p William Kennedy 1928 Maria Burton Carson 1961	**17** ☽ in ♏ ☽□☿ 8:55a ☽☌♂ 2:20p ☽△♀ 2:53p ☽□♅ 11:31p Don Zimmer 1931 David Caruso 1956	**18** ☽v/c 5:44p ☽→♐ 7:35p ☽☍♄ 8:12a ☽⚹☉ 5:44p ☽☍♃ 10:01p ☿⚹♇ 10:53p Alison Arngram 1962 Bobby Goldsboro 1941	**19** ☽ in ♐ ☽⚹♆ 7:19a ☉→♒ 4:16p ☽☌♇ 11:48p Katey Sagal 1954 **Sun enters Aquarius**	**20** ☽ in ♐ ☽v/c 10:18a ☿□♂ 1:05a ☽⚹☿ 3:28a ☽□♀ 6:15a ☽⚹♅ 10:18a ☉△♃ 8:59p David Lynch 1946 Sophie Rhys-Jones 1965
21 ☽→♑ 6:57a AQUARIUS No exact aspects Jack Nicklaus 1940 Charlotte Ross 1968	**22** ☽ in ♑ ☿☌♅ 11:35a ☽⚹♂ 6:35p Teddy Gentry 1950 Olga Markova 1974	**23** ☽v/c 7:38a ☽→♒ 7:43p ☽⚹♀ 0:06a ☽△♄ 7:38a ☽△♃ 10:09p Patrick Simmons 1950 Thomas R. Carper 1947	**24** New Moon 4♒37 5:07a ☽ in ♒ ☽☌☉ 5:07a ☽☌♆ 8:21a ♄SD 4:24p Mark Goodson 1915 **Chinese New Year**: Snake	**25** ☽ in ♒ ☽v/c 9:28p ☽□♂ 10:37a ☽☌♅ 12:20p ☿□♄ 1:35p ☉☌♆ 7:56p ♃SD 0:38a ☽□♄ 8:37p ☽⚹♇ 1:18a ☽☌☿ 9:28p Dean Jones 1931 Elizabeth Allen 1934	**26** ☽→♓ 8:39a ☽□♃ 11:03a ♀⚹♄ 9:25p Henry Jaglom 1943 Andrew Ridgeley 1963	**27** ☽ in ♓ ♂□♅ 3:10a ☽□♇ 2:01p Tracy Lawrence 1968 Skitch Henderson 1918
28 ☽v/c 11:48a ☽→♈ 8:35p ☽△♂ 1:58a ☽⚹♄ 8:52a ☽☌♀ 11:48a ☽⚹♃ 10:58p Marthe Keller 1945 Claes Oldenburg 1929	**29** ☽ in ♈ ☽⚹♆ 9:07a ☽⚹☉ 4:29p Edward Burns 1968 Claudine Longet 1942	**30** ☽ in ♈ ☽△♇ 1:11a ☽⚹♅ 11:54a Tammy Grimes 1934 Harold (Hal) Prince 1928	**31** ☽v/c 5:36a ☽→♉ 6:21a ☽⚹☿ 5:36a ☽□♆ 6:27p ☿→♓ 11:13p Kelly Lynch 1959 C. F. Martin, Sr. 1833	**JANUARY**		Moon goes void-of-course. Moon enters next sign. ☽v/c 4:35a ☽→♏ 11:02a Last Qtr. 26♎27 4:35a ☽□☉ 4:35a ☽□♆ 9:56p ♀□♇ 10:35p ♀△♂ 11:58p William Kennedy 19 Maria Burton Carson 1961 Daily aspects (when exact). Sign or Direction changes.

Pacific Standard Time

Day	☉	☿	♀	♂	♃	♄	♅	♆	♇	☊
1	13≈	00♉	29♓	23♏	01♊	24♉	20≈	07≈	15♐	14♌
2	14	01 R	00♈	24	01	24	20	07	15	14
3	15	01	01	24	01	24	20	07	15	14
4	16	01	02	25	01	24	21	07	15	14
5	17	00♉	03	26	02	24	21	07	15	14
6	18	30≈	04	26	02	24	21	07	15	14
7	19	29	05	27	02	24	21	07	15	14
8	20	29	06	28	02	24	21	07	15	14
9	21	28	07	28	02	24	21	07	15	14
10	22	27	07	29	02	25	21	07	15	13
11	23	26	08	29	02	25	21	07	15	13
12	24	25	09	30♏	03	25	21	07	15	13
13	25	23	09	00♐	03	25	21	07	15	13
14	26	22	10	01	03	25	21	07	15	13
15	27	21	11	01	03	25	21	07	15	13
16	28	20	11	02	03	25	21	07	15	13
17	29	19	12	02	03	25	21	07	15	13
18	00♓	18	13	02	03	25	21	07	15	13
19	01	17	13	03	03	25	21	07	15	13
20	02	17	14	03	03	25	21	07	15	13
21	03	16	14	04	03	25	22	07	15	13
22	04	16	15	04	03	25	22	07	15	13
23	05	16	15	05	03	25	22	07	15	13
24	06	15	16	05	03	25	22	07	15	13
25	07	15 D	16	06	03	25	22	07	15	13
26	08	16	16	06	03	25	22	07	15	13
27	09	16	16	07	04	25	22	07	15	13
28	10	16	16	07	04	25	22	07	15	13

Above are rounded to nearest whole degree. Positions more than 29°30′ round to 30° of one sign before 00° of the next sign. See pages 46-57 for a complete ephemeris.

FEBRUARY PLANTING DAYS
Above-ground crops: Best days: 5, 6, 23, 24   Good days: 1, 2, 28
Root crops & perennials: Best days: 13, 14   Good days: 11, 12, 18, 19

PLANETS VISIBLE IN THE MORNING SKY
Mercury beginning the 19th, and Mars.

PLANETS VISIBLE IN THE EVENING SKY
Mercury to the 7th, Venus, Jupiter, and Saturn.

AQUARIUS ♒   January 19 to February 18 "I KNOW"
A fixed, air sign of positive polarity.
SYMBOL: the water bearer—the energy bearer.
COLORS: iridescent blues.   RULING PLANETS: Saturn and Uranus.
RULES the circulation and the ankles.

FEBRUARY

AQUARIUS / PISCES

SUNDAY	MONDAY	TUESDAY	WEDNESDAY	THURSDAY	FRIDAY	SATURDAY

JANUARY 2001

S	M	T	W	T	F	S
	1	2	3	4	5	6
7	8	9	10	11	12	13
14	15	16	17	18	19	20
21	22	23	24	25	26	27
28	29	30	31			

MARCH 2001

S	M	T	W	T	F	S
				1	2	3
4	5	6	7	8	9	10
11	12	13	14	15	16	17
18	19	20	21	22	23	24
25	26	27	28	29	30	31

THURSDAY 1 — First Qtr. 12/547 6:02a
Jessica Savitch 1948
Anthony La Paglia 1959

FRIDAY 2 — Candlemas
Barry Diller 1942
Judith Viorst 1931

SATURDAY 3
Joey Bishop 1918
Melanie (Safka) 1947

SUNDAY 4 — ☽ in ♌
Nigel Bruce 1895
Mary Ann Pascal 1958

MONDAY 5 — ☽ in ♌
No exact aspects
Roger Staubach 1942
Elizabeth Swados 1951

TUESDAY 6
Axl Rose 1962
Claudio Arrau 1903

WEDNESDAY 7 — ☽ in ♍
Jason Adams 1963
Marilyn Cochran 1950

THURSDAY 8 — ☽ in ♍
Elizabeth Bishop 1911
Jim Greenspoon 1948

FRIDAY 9 — ☽ in ♍
Frank Frazetta 1928
Brendan Behan 1923

SATURDAY 10 — ☽ in ♎
Laura Dern 1967
Boris Pasternak 1890

SUNDAY 11 — ☽ in ♎
Roberto Moreno 1959
Brandy Norwood 1979

MONDAY 12
Joan Finney 1925
Robert A. Lutz 1932

TUESDAY 13 — ☽ in ♏
Jerry Springer 1944
Stockard Channing 1944

WEDNESDAY 14 — Full Moon 2/8/30 11:12p — St. Valentine's Day
Florence Henderson 1934

THURSDAY 15 — ☽ in ♏
Rusty Hamer 1947
Marisa Berenson 1947

FRIDAY 16 — ☽ in ♐
William Katt 1951
Gretchen Wyler 1932

SATURDAY 17
Mary Ann Mobley 1939
Billie Joe Armstrong 1972

SUNDAY 18 — ☽ in ♐ — Sun enters Pisces
Dennis DeYoung 1947

MONDAY 19 — Presidents' Day
Jill Krementz 1940

TUESDAY 20 — ☽ in ♑
Mike Leigh 1943
Sidney Poitier 1927

WEDNESDAY 21 — ☽ in ♒
William Baldwin 1963
Mary Chapin Carpenter 1958

THURSDAY 22 — Last Qtr. 2/6/30 7:23p
Jim Weah 1964
Arthur Schopenhauer 1788

FRIDAY 23 — ☽ in ♓
New Moon 4/4/47 0:21a
Allan Boesak 1945
Helena Sukova 1985

SATURDAY 24 — ☽ in ♈
Michel Legrand 1932
Sammy Kershaw 1958

SUNDAY 25 — ☽ in ♈
Davey Allison 1961
Catherine Larson 1965

MONDAY 26 — ☽ in ♉
David Wilson 1949
Marilyn Michaels 1944

TUESDAY 27 — ☽ in ♉
No exact aspects
Mary Frann 1943
Mardi Gras/Shrove Tues.

WEDNESDAY 28 — ☽ in ♊ — Ash Wednesday
Robert Sean Leonard 1969

Full Moon — Moon goes void-of-course. Moon enters next sign. Daily aspects (when exact). Sign or Direction changes.

Jason Adams 1963
Marilyn Cochran 1950

Pacific Standard Time

PISCES ♓

MARCH 2001

Day	☉	☿	♀	♂	♃	♄	♅	♆	♇	☊
1	11♓	16♒	17♈	08♐	03♊	25♉	22♒	08♒	15♐	13♋
2	12	17	17	08	03	25	22	08	15	12
3	13	17	17	09	03	25	22	08	15	12
4	14	18	17	09	04	25	22	08	15	12
5	15	19	18	10	04	26	22	08	15	12
6	16	19	18	10	04	26	22	08	15	12
7	17	20	18	11	04	26	22	08	15	12
8	18	21	18R	11	04	26	22	08	15	12
9	19	22	18	11	04	26	22	08	15	12
10	20	23	18	12	04	26	22	08	15	12
11	21	24	18	12	04	26	23	08	15	12
12	22	25	17	13	05	26	23	08	15	12
13	23	26	17	13	05	26	23	08	15	12
14	24	27	17	14	05	26	23	08	15	12
15	25	28	17	14	05	26	23	08	15	12
16	26	30	16	15	05	26	23	08	15	12
17	27	01♓	16	15	05	26	23	08	15R	12
18	28	02	16	15	05	27	23	08	15	12
19	29	03	15	16	06	27	23	08	15	12
20	00♈	05	15	16	06	27	23	08	15	12
21	01	06	14	17	06	27	23	08	15	11
22	02	08	14	17	06	27	23	08	15	11
23	03	09	13	18	06	27	23	08	15	11
24	04	10	13	18	06	27	23	08	15	11
25	05	12	12	18	07	27	23	08	15	11
26	06	13	12	19	07	27	23	08	15	11
27	07	15	11	19	07	27	23	08	15	11
28	08	16	10	20	07	27	23	08	15	11
29	09	18	10	20	07	28	23	08	15	11
30	10	20	09	20	07	28	23	08	15	11
31	11	21	08	21	08	28	23	08	15	11

Above are rounded to nearest whole degree. Positions more than 29°30' round to 30° of one sign before 00° of the next sign. See pages 46-57 for a complete ephemeris.

MARCH PLANTING DAYS
Above-ground crops: Best days: 4, 5, 31 Good days: 1, 27, 28
Root crops & perennials: Best days: 12, 13, 22, 23 Good: 10, 11, 17, 18

PLANETS VISIBLE IN THE MORNING SKY
Mercury and Mars.

PLANETS VISIBLE IN THE EVENING SKY
Venus to the 26th, Jupiter, and Saturn.

PISCES ♓ February 18 to March 20 "I BELIEVE"

A mutable, water sign of negative polarity.
SYMBOL: two fish swimming in opposite directions, and not seeing each other.
COLORS: sea greens.
RULING PLANET: Neptune.
RULES the feet.
KEYWORDS: compassionate, sensitive, imaginative, intuitive, escapist.

MARCH

SUNDAY	MONDAY	TUESDAY	WEDNESDAY	THURSDAY	FRIDAY	SATURDAY
MARCH		FEBRUARY 2001 S M T W T F S 1 2 3 4 5 6 7 8 9 10 11 12 13 14 15 16 17 18 19 20 21 22 23 24 25 26 27 28 APRIL 2001 S M T W T F S 1 2 3 4 5 6 7 8 9 10 11 12 13 14 15 16 17 18 19 20 21 22 23 24 25 26 27 28 29 30	Moon goes void-of-course. Moon enters next sign. ☽V/c 7:48p ☽→♑ 8:02p Last Qtr. 26♐19 12:45p ☽✱♅ 5:45a ☽□☉ 12:45p ☉✱♄ 1:42p ☽✱☿ 7:48p ☿→♓ 10:05p Flavor Flav 1959 Victor Garber 1949 Daily aspects (when exact). Sign or Direction changes.	**1** ☽V/c 10:57a ☽→♊ 7:36p ☽□♅ 4:59a ♂✱♆ 7:42a ☽☌♄ 10:57a David Niven 1910 Dirk Benedict 1945	☽ in ♊ First Qtr. 12♊33 6:03p ☽☌♃ 1:33a ☽△♆ 9:10a ☽☍♂ 10:03a ☽□☉ 6:03p ☽☍♇ 10:44p Peter Straub 1943 Jennifer Jones 1919	**3** ☽ in ♊ ☽V/c 10:45a ☽△☿ 1:59a ☽✱♀ 2:03a ☿✱♀ 4:36a ☽△♅ 10:45a Jennifer Warnes 1947 Robyn Hitchcock 1953
4 ☽→♋ 0:24a PISCES No exact aspects Emilio Estefan 1953 Catherine O'Hara 1954	**5** ☽ in ♋ ☽V/c 7:10p ☽△☉ 1:33a ☽□♀ 5:54a ☉□♇ 10:11a ☽✱♄ 7:10p Samantha Eggar 1939 James B. Sikking 1934	**6** ☽→♌ 2:30a ☽✱♃ 8:41a ☽☍♆ 2:58p ☽△♂ 6:56p Tom Arnold 1959 Jackie Zeman 1953	**7** ☽ in ♌ ☽V/c 7:50p ☽△♇ 3:09a ☽△♀ 7:04a ☽☍☿ 10:55a ☽☍♅ 2:28p ☽□♄ 7:50p Taylor Dayne 1962 Anthony Armstrong-Jones 1930	**8** ☽→♍ 2:44a ☽□♃ 9:12a ♀SR 5:07p ☽□♂ 8:26p Carol Bayer Sager 1947 **Internat'l. Women's Day**	☽ in ♍ ☽V/c 8:01p Full Moon 19♍12 9:23a ☽□♇ 3:04a ☽☍☉ 9:23a ☽△♄ 8:01p **Purim** Michael Kinsley 1951 Juliette Binoche 1964	**10** ☽→♎ 2:47a ☿☌♅ 1:51a ☽△♃ 9:49a ☽△♆ 3:31p ☽✱♂ 10:32p Bob Greene 1947 Linda Jezek 1960
11 ☽ in ♎ ☽V/c 6:44p ☽✱♇ 3:49a ☽☍♀ 7:42a ☽△♅ 3:59p ☽△☿ 6:44p Harold Wilson 1916 Bobby McFerrin 1950	**12** ☽→♏ 4:42a ☽□♆ 6:21p Lloyd Dobbins 1936 Courtney B. Vance 1960	**13** ☽ in ♏ ☿□♄ 2:30p ☽□♅ 8:44p ☽△☉ 10:45p Lyn St. James 1947 Glenne Headly 1959	**14** ☽V/c 4:17a ☽→♐ 10:16a ☽☍♄ 3:10a ☽□☿ 4:17a ☽☍♃ 7:29p Steve Kanaly 1946 Marguerite DeAngeli 1889	**15** ☽ in ♐ ☽✱♆ 1:10a ☽☌♂ 1:01p ☽☌♇ 3:12p ☽△♀ 5:57p Mike Love 1941 Macdonald Carey 1913	☽V/c 7:48p ☽→♑ 8:02p Last Qtr. 26♐19 12:45p ☽✱♅ 5:45a ☽□☉ 12:45p ☉✱♄ 1:42p ☽✱☿ 7:48p ☿→♓ 10:05p Flavor Flav 1959 Victor Garber 1949	**17** ☽ in ♑ ♇SR 6:36p **St. Patrick's Day** Oksana Gritschuk 1971
18 ☽ in ♑ ♂☌♇ 3:45a ☽□♀ 3:55a ♀△♂ 9:29p James McMurtry 1962 Grover Cleveland 1837	**19** ☽V/c 6:40a ☽→♒ 8:36a ☽△♄ 1:38a ☽✱☉ 6:40a ♀△♇ 3:31p ☽△♃ 8:09p Irving Wallace 1916 Phyllis Newman 1935	**20** ☽ in ♒ ☽☌♆ 1:03a ☉→♈ 5:31a ☽✱♀ 2:49p ☽✱♇ 3:42p ☽✱♂ 5:57p **Vernal Equinox** **Sun enters Aries**	**21** ☽V/c 3:03p ☽→♓ 9:28p ☽☌♅ 7:24a ☿□♃ 11:41a ☽□♄ 3:03p Russ Meyer 1922 Kathleen Widdoes 1939	**22** ☽ in ♓ ARIES ☽□♃ 9:37a ☽☌☿ 12:08p Jeremy Clyde 1944 Stephanie Mills 1957	**23** ☽ in ♓ ☽□♇ 3:53a ☽□♂ 8:12a Marty Allen 1922 Mark Rydell 1934	☽V/c 2:58a ☽→♈ 8:44a New Moon 4♈28 5:21p ☽✱♄ 2:58a ☽☌☉ 5:21p ☽✱♃ 9:13p Star Jones 1962 Edward Weston 1886
25 ☽ in ♈ ☽✱♆ 0:33a ☽☌♀ 8:24a ☽△♇ 2:02p ☽△♂ 8:06p Nick Lowe 1949 Mary Gross 1953	**26** ☽V/c 5:10a ☽→♉ 5:51p ☽✱♅ 5:10a Martin Short 1950 Bob Woodard 1943	**27** ☽ in ♉ ☉✱♃ 2:57a ☽□♆ 9:12a ☽✱☿ 10:04p ☿□♇ 10:28p Mariah Carey 1971 Derrick McKenzie 1964	**28** ☽ in ♉ ☽V/c 8:29p ☽□♅ 12:57p ☉✱♆ 1:55p ☽☌♄ 8:29p Dirk Bogarde 1920 Lon Warneke 1909	**29** ☽→♊ 1:01a ☽☌♃ 2:05p ☽△♆ 3:58p ☽✱☉ 6:00p ☽✱♀ 6:17p ☉☌♀ 8:16p Lara Flynn Boyle 1970 Christopher Lambert 1957	**30** ☽ in ♊ ☽V/c 6:54p ☽☍♇ 4:21a ☽□☿ 11:23a ☽☍♂ 1:16p ☽△♅ 6:54p John Astin 1930 Robbie Coltrane 1950	**31** ☽→♋ 6:23a ☿□♂ 7:36a ♀✱♆ 5:30p ☽□♀ 8:45p John Jakes 1932 Anne Howard 1960

Pacific Standard Time

Day	☉	☿	♀	♂	♃	♄	♅	♆	♇	☊
1	12♈	23♓	08♈R	21♐	08♊	28♉	24♒	08♒	15♐R	11♋
2	13	24	07	21	08	28	24	08	15	11
3	14	26	07	22	08	28	24	08	15	11
4	15	28	06	22	08	28	24	08	15	11
5	16	00♈	05	23	09	28	24	08	15	11
6	17	01	04	23	09	28	24	08	15	11
7	18	03	03	23	09	29	24	08	15	11
8	19	05	04	24	09	29	24	09	15	10
9	20	07	04	24	10	29	24	09	15	10
10	21	08	03	24	10	29	24	09	15	10
11	22	10	03	25	10	29	24	09	15	10
12	23	12	02	25	11	30	24	09	15	10
13	24	14	02	25	11	30	24	09	15	10
14	25	16	02	25	12	00♊	24	09	15	10
15	26	18	02	26	12	00	24	09	15	10
16	27	20	02	26	12	00	24	09	15	10
17	28	22	02	26	13	00	24	09	15	10
18	29	24	02 D	27	13	01	24	09	15	10
19	30	26	01	27	13	01	24	09	15	10
20	01♉	28	01	27	14	01	24	09	15	09
21	02	00♉	01	27	14	01	24	09	15	09
22	03	02	02	28	12	01	24	09	15	09
23	04	04	02	28	12	01	24	09	15	09
24	05	05	02	28	12	01	24	09	15	09
25	06	07	03	28	13	01	25	09	15	09
26	07	09	03	28	13	01	25	09	15	09
27	08	11	04	28	13	01	25	09	15	09
28	09	13	04	28	13	01	25	09	15	09
29	10	14	05	28	13	01	25	09	09	09
30	11	16	05	28	13	01	25	09	09	09

Above are rounded to nearest whole degree. Positions more than 29°30' round to 30° of one sign before 00° of the next sign. See pages 46-57 for a complete ephemeris.

APRIL PLANTING DAYS
Above-ground crops:
Best days: 1, 28, 29   Good days: 7, 23, 24
Root crops/perennials: Best days: 9, 10, 18-20   Good days: 8, 13-15
PLANETS VISIBLE IN THE MORNING SKY
Mercury to the 15th, Venus from the 4th, and Mars.
PLANETS VISIBLE IN THE EVENING SKY
Jupiter and Saturn.

ARIES ♈   March 20 to April 19 "I AM"
A cardinal, fire sign of positive polarity.
SYMBOL: the ram, lowering its head and blindly charging through.
COLORS: reds.   RULING PLANET: Mars.   RULES the head.
KEYWORDS: aggressive, straightforward, impulsive, adventurous, active.

APRIL

SUNDAY	MONDAY	TUESDAY	WEDNESDAY	THURSDAY	FRIDAY	SATURDAY
1 ☽ in ♋ First Qtr. 11♋46 3:49a ☽□☉ 3:49a ♀*♃ 4:18p ☽△☿ 11:19p **April Fools' Day** **Daylight Saving Time begins**	**2** ☽v/c 7:26a ☽→♌ 10:54a ARIES ☽*♄ 7:26a ☽△♀ 10:42p Emile Zola 1840 Jack Webb 1920	**3** ☽ in ♌ ☽*♃ 0:22a ☽☍♆ 1:00a ☽△☉ 10:22a ☽△♇ 12:20p ☽△♂ 11:19p Lawton Chiles 1930 David Hyde Pierce 1959	**4** ☽v/c 9:46a ☽→♍ 12:46p ☽☍♅ 2:18a ☽□♄ 9:46a ☉△♇ 3:03p ☿*♄ 11:40p Gail Davies 1948 Anthony Clark 1963	**5** ☽ in ♍ ☽□♃ 2:33a ♃△♆ 7:26a ☽□♇ 1:39p Jane Asher 1946 Arthur Hailey 1920	**6** ☽v/c 11:18a ☽→♎ 1:57p ☿→♈ 0:14a ☽□♂ 1:42a ☽△♄ 11:18a ☽☍☿ 3:49p ☽☍♀ 9:54p Janet Lynn 1953 George Reeves 1914	**7** ☽ in ♎ Full Moon 18♎22 8:22p ☽△♆ 3:55a ☽△♃ 4:26a ☽*♇ 3:01p ☽☍☉ 8:22p Posh Spice 1974 Daniel Ellsberg 1931
8 ☽v/c 5:30a ☽→♏ 4:01p ☽*♂ 4:33a ☽△♅ 5:30a ☿☌♀ 8:25a **Passover** **Palm Sunday** Patricia Arquette 1968	**9** ☽ in ♏ ☽□♆ 6:39a Hal Ketchum 1953 Paulina Porizkova 1965	**10** ☽v/c 6:43p ☽→♐ 8:47p ♂*♅ 6:27a ☽□♅ 9:44a ☿*♆ 6:03p ☽☍♄ 6:43p Brian Setzer 1959 Max Von Sydow 1929	**11** ☽ in ♐ ☽△♀ 2:18a ☿*♃ 7:13a ☽*♆ 12:30p ☽☍♃ 2:29p ☽△☿ 3:36p John Milius 1944 Howard W. Koch 1916	**12** ☽ in ♐ ☽v/c 6:56p ☽☌♇ 0:46a ☽△☉ 3:58p ☽*♅ 5:40p ☽☌♂ 6:56p Claire Danes 1979 Herbie Hancock 1940	**13** ☽→♑ 5:21a ☽□♀ 9:51a ☉*♅ 2:25p **Good Friday** Edward Fox 1937 Ben Nighthorse Campbell 1933	**14** ☽ in ♑ ☿△♇ 4:38a ☽□☿ 12:22p ☉△♂ 7:32p **Pan American Day** Sarah Michelle Gellar 1977
15 ☽v/c 4:00p ☽→♒ 5:11p Last Qtr. 25♑43 8:31a ☽□☉ 8:31a ☽△♄ 4:00p ☽*♀ 8:48p **Easter Sunday** Samatha Fox 1966	**16** ☽ in ♒ ☽☌♆ 10:41a ☽△♃ 2:41p ☽*♇ 11:43p Edie Adams 1929 Martin Lawrence 1965	**17** ☽ in ♒ ☽*☿ 1:20p ☽☌♅ 6:11p ☽*♂ 9:55p Teri Austin 1959 Don Kirshner 1934	**18** ☽v/c 5:26a ☽→♓ 6:00a ☽*☉ 2:49a ☽□♄ 5:26a ☿*♅ 5:53p Eric Roberts 1956 Jane Leeves 1963	**19** ☽ in ♓ ☽□♃ 4:13a ☽□♇ 11:56a ☉→♉ 5:36p ☿△♂ 8:22p ♀SD 9:34p Hugh O'Brian 1930 **Sun enters Taurus**	**20** ☽v/c 10:40a ☽→♈ 5:18p ☽□♂ 10:40a ♄→♊ 2:59p ☽*♄ 5:19p ☽☌♀ 8:09p Carmen Electra 1972 Adrian Fernandez 1965	**21** ☽ in ♈ ☽*♆ 9:58a ☿→♉ 1:08p ☽*♃ 3:31p ☽△♇ 9:52p Robert Smith 1959 Silvana Mangano 1930
22 ☽ in ♈ ☽v/c 8:34p ☽*♅ 3:22p ☽△♂ 8:34p **Earth Day** Greg Moore 1975 Deane Beman 1938	**23** ☽→♉ 1:56a New Moon 3♉32 8:26a ☉☌☿ 2:25a ☽☌☉ 8:26a ☽☌☿ 9:04a ☽□♆ 5:53p Judy Davis 1955 Leonardo da Vinci 1452	**24** ☽ in ♉ ☽v/c 10:08p TAURUS ☽□♅ 10:08p Sue Grafton 1940 Michael O'Keefe 1955	**25** ☽→♊ 8:11a ☽☌♄ 9:12a ☽*♀ 11:50a ☿□♆ 3:23p ☽△♆ 11:37p **Secretary's Day** Johan Cruyff 1947	**26** ☽ in ♊ ☽☌♃ 6:22a ☽☍♇ 10:26a Roger Taylor 1960 Martha Rockwell 1944	**27** ☽v/c 9:12a ☽→♋ 12:49p ☽△♅ 3:07a ☽☍♂ 9:12a ☽□♀ 5:20p Ann Peebles 1947 Cuba Gooding 1944	**28** ☽ in ♋ ☽v/c 2:53p ☽*☉ 2:58a ☽*☿ 2:53p ☉□♆ 4:50p Chris Young 1971 Nancy Grahn 1959
29 ☽→♌ 4:25p ☽*♄ 6:18p ☽△♀ 10:02p Otis Rush 1934 Chad Little 1963	**30** ☽ in ♌ First Qtr. 10♌25 10:08a ☽☍♆ 7:19a ☽□☉ 10:08a ☽*♃ 3:20p ☽△♇ 5:32p Paul Gross 1959 Jane Campion 1954		**APRIL**		Moon goes void-of-course. Moon enters next sign. ☽v/c 4:00p ☽→♒ 5:11p Last Qtr. 25♑43 8:31a ☽□☉ 8:31a ☽△♄ 4:00p ☽*♀ 8:48p Easter Sunday Samatha Fox 1966 Daily aspects (when exact). Sign or Direction changes.	(see mini calendars below)

MARCH 2001

S	M	T	W	T	F	S
				1	2	3
4	5	6	7	8	9	10
11	12	13	14	15	16	17
18	19	20	21	22	23	24
25	26	27	28	29	30	31

MAY 2001

S	M	T	W	T	F	S
		1	2	3	4	5
6	7	8	9	10	11	12
13	14	15	16	17	18	19
20	21	22	23	24	25	26
27	28	29	30	31		

Pacific Daylight Saving Time begins at 2:00am April 1st. **Turn clocks ahead one hour.**

TAURUS ♉

MAY 2001

Day	☉	☿	♀	♂	♃	♄	♅	♆	♇	☊
1	12♉	22♉	04♈	28♐	14♊	01♊	25♒	09♒	15R	09♋
2	13	24	04	29	14	01	25	09	15♐	09
3	14	26	05	29	14	02	25	09	15	09
4	15	28	05	29	14	02	25	09	15	09
5	16	30	06	29	15	02	25	09	15	09
6	17	02♊	06	29	15	02	25	09	15	09
7	17	03	07	29	15	02	25	09	15	09
8	18	05	07	29	15	02	25	09	15	09
9	19	07	08	29	15	02	25	09	15	09
10	20	09	09	29	16	02	25	09R	15	09
11	21	10	09	29R	16	03	25	09	15	09
12	22	12	10	29	16	03	25	09	15	09
13	23	13	11	29	16	03	25	09	14	09
14	24	15	11	29	17	03	25	09	14	09
15	25	16	12	29	17	03	25	09	14	09
16	26	18	13	29	17	03	25	09	14	08
17	27	19	13	29	17	03	25	09	14	08
18	28	20	14	29	17	04	25	09	14	08
19	29	21	15	29	18	04	25	09	14	08
20	00♊	22	16	28	18	04	25	09	14	08
21	01	23	16	28	18	04	25	09	14	08
22	02	24	17	28	18	04	25	09	14	08
23	03	25	18	28	19	04	25	09	14	08
24	04	26	19	28	19	04	25	09	14	08
25	05	27	20	28	19	04	25	09	14	08
26	06	27	21	28	19	05	25	09	14	08
27	07	28	21	27	19	05	25	09	14	08
28	08	28	22	27	20	05	25	09	14	08
29	09	29	23	27	20	05	25R	09	14	08
30	10	29	24	27	20	05	25	09	14	08
31	11	30	25	26	20	05	25	09	14	08

Above are rounded to nearest whole degree. Positions more than 29°30' round to 30° of one sign before 00° of the next sign. See pages 46-57 for a complete ephemeris.

MAY PLANTING DAYS
Above-ground crops: Best days: 6, 25, 26   Good days: 4, 5, 31
Root crops/perennials: Best days: 7, 16, 17   Good: 11, 12, 20, 21, 22

PLANETS VISIBLE IN THE MORNING SKY
Venus and Mars.

PLANETS VISIBLE IN THE EVENING SKY
Mercury, Jupiter, and Saturn to the 7th. **Do not confuse** Saturn with Mercury the first week. Mercury is brighter. Also, **do not confuse** Jupiter with Mercury mid-month. Jupiter is brighter.

TAURUS ♉ April 19 to May 20 "I HAVE"

A fixed, earth sign of negative polarity.
SYMBOL: the bull. COLORS: pink and blue. RULING PLANET: Venus.
RULES the throat, cerebellum and back part of the brain.
KEYWORDS: possessive, stable, determined, practical, sensual.

MAY

SUNDAY	MONDAY	TUESDAY	WEDNESDAY	THURSDAY	FRIDAY	SATURDAY
	MAY	**1** — May Day; D'Arcy 1968; Charlie Schlatter 1966	**2** — Lorenzo Music 1937; Elizabeth Berridge 1962	**3** — Jill Berard 1930; Dave Dudley 1928	**4** — Mary McDonough 1961; Maynard Ferguson 1928	**5** — Cinco de Mayo; Jean-Pierre Léaud 1944
6 — Mark Bryan 1967; Roma Downey 1964	**7** — Full Moon 6:53a; Tim Roth 1961; Robert Zemeckis 1952	**8** — James Mitchum 1941; Thomas Pynchon 1937	**9** — Tommy Roe 1946; Alan Bennett 1934	**10** — Teri Copley 1961; Meg Foster 1948	**11** — Randy Quaid 1950; Mark Herndon 1955	**12** — Kix Brooks 1955; Ving Rhames 1961
13 — Mother's Day; Stephen Donaldson 1947	**14** — Bill Danoff 1946; Michael E. Knight 1959	**15** — Last Qtr 24°08 3:11a; Eddy Arnold 1918; Wavy Gravy 1936	**16** — New Moon 23°03 7:46p; Dan Coats 1943; Tracy Gold 1969	**17** — Enya 1961; Fiona Hutchison 1960	**18** — Candice Azzara 1947; Dwayne Hickman 1934	**19** — James Lehrer 1934; Lorraine Hansberry 1930
20 — Sun enters Gemini; Susan Cowsill 1960; Leo Sayer 1948	**21** — Victoria Day; Raymond Burr 1917	**22** — Ed Fry 1958; Charles Aznavour 1924	**23** — Ilia Kulik 1977; Judy Rodman 1951	**24** — Ascension Day; Alfred Molina 1953	**25** — Lauryn Hill 1975; Anne Heche 1969	**26**
27 — Siouxsie Sioux 1957; Henry Kissinger 1923	**28** — Shavuot; Memorial Day; Rowland Gift 1962	**29** — Adrian Paul 1959; Helmut Berger 1944	**30** — First Qtr 8°05 3:09p; Ralph Carter 1961; Stephen Tobolowsky 1951	**31** — Denholm Elliott 1922; Alexander Pope 1688		

TAURUS · GEMINI

Pacific Daylight Saving Time

Legend:

- Last Qtr [icon] — D v/c 11:53a · D→♈ 2:10p
- New Moon
- First Qtr
- Full Moon

Moon goes void-of-course. Moon enters next sign.
Daily aspects (when exact). Sign or Direction changes.

Example: Eddy Arnold 1918 / Wavy Gravy 1936 — Last Qtr 24°08 3:11a

---

APRIL 2001

S	M	T	W	T	F	S
1	2	3	4	5	6	7
8	9	10	11	12	13	14
15	16	17	18	19	20	21
22	23	24	25	26	27	28
29	30					

JUNE 2001

S	M	T	W	T	F	S
					1	2
3	4	5	6	7	8	9
10	11	12	13	14	15	16
17	18	19	20	21	22	23
24	25	26	27	28	29	30

Day	☉	☿	♀	♂	♃	♄	♅	♆	♇	☊
1	12♊	30♊	26♈	26♐	21♊	05♊	25♒R	09♒R	14♐R	08♋R
2	12	30	27	26♐	21	06	25	09	14♐	08
3	13	30R	28	25	21	06	25	09	14	07
4	14	30	29	25	22	06	25	09	14	07
5	15	30	01♉	24	22	06	25	09	14	07
6	16	30	02	24	23	06	25	09	14	07
7	17	29	03	23	23	07	25	09	14	07
8	18	01♋	04	23	24	07	25	09	14	07
9	19	01	05	22	24	07	25	09	14	07
10	20	00	06	21	24	07	25	09	14	06
11	21	29	07	21	25	07	25	09	14	06
12	22	29	08	20	25	07	25	08	13	06
13	23	29	09	20	25	08	25	08	13	06
14	24	24	10	19	26	08	25	08	13	06
15	25	26	11	19	26	08	25	08	13	06
16	26	26	12	18	26	08	25	08	13	06
17	27	27	19	24	07	08	25	08	13	06
18	28	24	20	23	07	08	25	08	13	06
19	29	29	21	23	07	08	25	08	13	06
20	00♋	01♋S	21	22	18	08	24	08	13	06
21	01	02	23	18	27	09	24	08	13	06
22	02	03	24	18	27	09	24	08	13	06
23	03	18♊D	25	18	27	09	24	08	13	06
24	04	22	19	19	26	08	25	08	13	06
25	04	04	21	19	26	08	25	08	13	06
26	05	05	21	19	26	08	25	08	13	06
27	06	06	22	18	27	09	24	08	13	06
28	07	07	23	18	27	09	24	08	13	06
29	08	09	24	18	27	09	24	08	13	06
30	09	11	25	18	27	09	24	08	13	06

Above are rounded to nearest whole degree. Positions more than 29°30' round to 30° of one sign before 00° of the next sign. See pages 46-57 for a complete ephemeris.

JUNE PLANTING DAYS
Above-ground crops:
    Best days: 2, 3, 4, 21, 22, 30   Good days: 1, 27, 28, 29
Root crops/perennials: Best days: 12, 13   Good days: 7, 8, 17, 18

PLANETS VISIBLE IN THE MORNING SKY
    Mercury from 26th, Venus, Mars to the 13th, Jupiter from 29th, and Saturn from 13th.

PLANETS VISIBLE IN THE EVENING SKY
    Mercury to the 7th, Mars beginning the 13th.

GEMINI ♊ May 20 to June 21 "I THINK"

A mutable, air sign with neutral polarity.
SYMBOL: the twins, Castor and Pollux.
COLORS: a variety—just about all!   RULING PLANET: Mercury.
RULES: the nervous system, hands, shoulders, arms and lungs.
KEYWORDS: versatile, flexible, sociable, dualistic, curious, inquisitive.

SUNDAY	MONDAY	TUESDAY	WEDNESDAY	THURSDAY	FRIDAY	SATURDAY
JUNE		Moon goes void-of-course. Moon enters next sign. ☽v/c 3:12a ☽→♎ 9:11a First Qtr. 6♎30 8:20p ☽□♃ 3:12a ☽□☉ 8:20p ☿SD 10:49p ☽△♆ 11:15p ☽△♄ 11:58p Lorrie Morgan 1959 Johnny Benson 1963 Daily aspects (when exact). Sign or Direction changes.	MAY 2001 S M T W T F S 1 2 3 4 5 6 7 8 9 10 11 12 13 14 15 16 17 18 19 20 21 22 23 24 25 26 27 28 29 30 31 JULY 2001 S M T W T F S 1 2 3 4 5 6 7 8 9 10 11 12 13 14 15 16 17 18 19 20 21 22 23 24 25 26 27 28 29 30 31		**1** ☽ in ♎ ☽✶♇ 3:53a ☽△♃ 3:25p ☽△♅ 10:49p Pat Boone 1934 Colleen McCullough 1937	**2** ☽v/c 7:41a ☽→♏ 7:56a ♀△♂ 0:03a ☽✶♂ 1:07a ☽☍♀ 1:13a ☽△☿ 7:41a ☽□♆ 11:17p Milo O'Shea 1926 Larry Clark Robinson 1951
3 ☽ in ♏ ☿SR 10:22p **Whit Sunday/Pentecost** Kathleen E. Woodiwiss 1939	**4** ☽v/c 4:29a ☽→♐ 1:58p ☽□♅ 4:29a ☉☍♇ 4:50a Scott Wolf 1968 Dennis Weaver 1924	**5** ☽ in ♐ Full Moon 15♐26 6:39p ☽☍♄ 0:35a ☽✶♆ 5:53a ☽☌♇ 3:45p ☽☍☉ 6:39p ☿✶♀ 10:41p Karen Sillas 1965 Spalding Gray 1941	**6** ☽v/c 9:41p ☽→♑ 10:23p ☽v/c 11:57p ☽✶♅ 12:26p ☽☌♂ 12:37p ♂✶♅ 8:54p ♀→♉ 3:25a ☽☍☿ 9:41p ☽☍♃ 6:28a ☽△♀ 11:57p Roy Innis 1934 Lorrie Morgan 1959	**7** ☽v/c in ♑ No exact aspects Dolores Gray 1930 Elizabeth Bowen 1899	**8** ☽v/c in ♑ No exact aspects Sonia Braga 1950 Juliana Marguiles 1967	**9** ☽→♒ 9:20a ☽□♀ 4:06p ☽△♄ 10:08p Dean Felber 1967 Natalie Portman 1981
10 ☽ in ♒ ☽☌♆ 2:28a ☽✶♇ 12:59p Philip Caputo 1941 Elisabeth Shue 1963	**11** ☽v/c 5:39p ☽→♓ 9:53p ☽△☉ 2:42a ☽△♃ 7:23a ☽✶♂ 8:35a ☽☌♅ 11:17a ☽△☿ 5:39p Frank Beard 1949 Peter Bergman 1953	**12** ☽ in ♓ ♂☍♃ 10:01a ☽✶♀ 10:11a ☽□♄ 11:27a Gwen Torrence 1965 Samuel Z. Arkoff 1918	**13** ☽ in ♓ Last Qtr. 23♓09 8:28p ☽□♇ 1:31a ☉☍♂ 10:46a ☽□♂ 7:28p ☽□☉ 8:28p ☽□♃ 9:02p Jamie Walters 1969 Malcolm McDowell 1943	**14** ☽v/c 3:26a ☽→♈ 10:03a ☽□☿ 3:26a ☉☌♃ 5:38a ♀□♆ 7:46p ☽✶♄ 11:50p **Flag Day** Gene Barry 1919 John Edgar Wideman 1941	**15** ☽ in ♈ ☽✶♆ 2:37a ☉△♅ 11:57a ☽△♇ 12:36p Harry Nilsson 1942 Neil Patrick Harris 1973	**16** ☽v/c 11:32a ☽→♉ 7:39p ☽△♂ 4:23a ☉☌☿ 6:26a ☽✶♃ 8:24a ☽✶♅ 9:44a ☽✶☿ 10:57a ☽✶☉ 11:32a Wallis Simpson 1896 Yasmine Bleeth 1968
17 ☽ in ♉ ☽□♆ 11:11a ☿△♅ 3:08p ☽☌♀ 4:31p **Father's Day** Greg Kinnear 1964 Barry Manilow 1946	**18** ☽ in ♉ ☽v/c 4:21p ☿☌♃ 3:12a ☽□♅ 4:21p Sylvia Porter 1913 E. G. Marshall 1910	**19** ☽→♊ 1:42a ♃△♅ 5:17a ☽●♄ 2:52p ☽△♆ 4:12p Andy Lauer 1965 Doug Stone 1956	**20** ☽ in ♊ ☽v/c 8:24p ☽☍♇ 0:57a ☽☍♂ 12:44p ☽☌☿ 5:10p ☽△♅ 7:44p ☽☌♃ 8:24p Brian Wilson 1942 Michael Anthony 1955	**21** ☽→♋ 4:41a  **Solar Eclipse** New Moon 0♋10 4:58a ☉→♋ 0:38a ☽●☉ 4:58a **Summer Solstice** **Sun enters Cancer**	**22** ☽ in ♋ ☽v/c 7:11a ☽✶♀ 7:11a Britt Hume 1943 Michael Lerner 1941	**23** ☽→♌ 5:55a ☽✶♄ 7:08p ☽☍♆ 7:25p Wilma Rudolph 1940 Karin Gustafson 1959
24 ☽ in ♌ ☽△♇ 3:45a ☽□♀ 11:52a ☽△♂ 1:16p ☽✶☿ 5:15p ☽☍♅ 10:01p Fred Hoyle 1915 George E. Pataki 1945	**25** ☽v/c 0:22a ☽→♍ 6:57a ♄△♆ 0:17a ☽✶♃ 0:22a ☽✶☉ 2:09p ☽□♄ 8:48p George Abbott 1887 Phyllis George Brown 1949	**26** ☽ in ♍ ☽□♇ 5:05a ☽□♂ 1:57p ☽△♀ 5:27p ☽□☿ 6:28p Colin Wilson 1931 Charles Robb 1939	**27** ☽v/c 3:12a ☽→♎ 9:11a First Qtr. 6♎30 8:20p ☽□♃ 3:12a ☽□☉ 8:20p ☿SD 10:49p ☽△♆ 11:15p ☽△♄ 11:58p Lorrie Morgan 1959 Johnny Benson 1963	**28** ☽ in ♎ ☽✶♇ 8:03a ☽✶♂ 4:22p ☽△☿ 10:04p King Henry VIII 1491 Danielle Brisebois 1969	**29** ☽v/c 8:07a ☽→♏ 1:28p ☽△♅ 3:39a ☽△♃ 8:07a Jeff Burton 1967 Sharon Lawrence 1962	**30** ☽ in ♏ ☽□♆ 4:07a ☽△☉ 5:13a ♀□♅ 5:46a Nancy Dussault 1936 William Zeckendorf 1905

Pacific Daylight Saving Time

JULY 2001

Above are rounded to nearest whole degree. Positions more than 29°30' round to 30° of one sign before 00' of the next sign. See pages 46-57 for a complete ephemeris.

Day	☉	☿	♀	♂	♃	♄	♅	♆	♇	☊
1	10♋	22♊R	26♉	17♐R	28♊	09♊	24♒R	08♒R	13♐R	06♋
2	11	22	27	17	28	09	24	08	13	06
3	12	23	29	17	28	09	24	08	13	06
4	13	24	00♊	16	28	10	24	08	13	06
5	14	24	01	16	29	10	24	08	13	06
6	15	25	03	16	29	10	24	08	13	06
7	16	25	04	16	29	10	24	08	13	06
8	17	27	05	16	29	10	24	08	13	06
9	18	28	07	16	30	11	24	08	13	05
10	19	29	08	15	30	11	24	08	13	05
11	20	01♋	09	15	30	11	24	08	13	05
12	21	03	10	15D	00♋	11	24	08	13	05
13	22	05	12	15	01	11	24	08	13	05
14	23	07	13	15	01	11	24	08	13	05
15	24	09	15	15	01	11	24	08	13	05
16	25	11	16	15	01	11	24	08	13	05
17	26	14	17	15	02	11	24	08	13	05
18	27	16	19	15	02	11	24	08	13	05
19	28	19	20	15D	02	11	24	08	13	05
20	29	21	21	15	03	11	24	07	13	05
21	00♌	24	23	15	03	12	24	07	13	05
22	00♌	26	24	15	03	12	24	07	13	05
23	01	01♌	25	15	03	12	24	07	13	05
24	02	03	26	15	04	12	24	07	13	05
25	03	05	28	16	04	12	24	07	13	05
26	04	08	29	16	04	12	23	07	13	05
27	05	12	00♋	16	04	12	23	07	13	05
28	06	14	01♋	16	04	12	23	07	13	05
29	07	17	27	16	04	12	24	07	13	05
30	08	01♌	28	16	04	12	23	07	13	05
31	09	03	29	16	05	11	23	07	13	04

JULY PLANTING DAYS
Above-ground crops: Best days: 1, 27, 28 Good: 4, 25, 26, 31
Root crops/perennials: Best days: 9, 10, 11, 19, 20 Good: 5, 6, 14, 15

PLANETS VISIBLE IN THE MORNING SKY
Mercury the 29th, Venus, Jupiter, and Saturn. **Do not confuse** Jupiter with Mercury around mid-month. Jupiter is brighter. **Do not confuse** Saturn with Venus during middle of month. Venus is brighter.

PLANET VISIBLE IN THE EVENING SKY
Mars.

CANCER ♋ June 21 to July 22 "I FEEL"

A cardinal, water sign of negative polarity.
SYMBOL: the crab. RULES the breasts, stomach and solar plexus.
COLORS: silver and soft shades. RULING PLANET: the Moon.
KEYWORDS: fertile, domestic, nurturing, emotional, sensitive, evasive.

JULY

SUNDAY	MONDAY	TUESDAY	WEDNESDAY	THURSDAY	FRIDAY	SATURDAY
1 ☽v/c 12:25p ☽→♐ 8:13p CANCER ☽□♅ 9:50a ☽☍♀ 12:25p **Canada Day** James Cotton 1935 Lorna Patterson 1957	**2** ☽ in ♐ ☽✶♆ 11:25a ☽☍♄ 1:26p ☽☌♇ 9:03p Jerry Hall 1956 Ed Bullins 1935	**3** ☽ in ♐ ☽☌♂ 4:16a ☽☍☿ 2:59p ☽✶♅ 6:26p Hunter Tylo 1962 Fontella Bass 1940	**4** ☽v/c 1:36a ☽→♑ 5:21a ☽☍♃ 1:36a **U.S. Independence Day** George Steinbrenner 1930	**5** ☽ in ♑ ☽v/c 8:04a **Lunar Eclipse** Full Moon 13♑39 8:04a ☽⚻☉ 8:04a ♀→♊ 9:44a Marc Cohn 1959 Shirley Knight 1936	**6** ☽→♒ 4:33p ☿△♅ 1:42p ☽△♀ 7:37p Burt Ward 1945 Geoffry Rush 1951	**7** ☽ in ♒ ☽☌♆ 8:35a ☽△♄ 12:05p ☽✶♇ 6:50p Robert A. Heinlein 1907 David McCullough 1933
8 ☽ in ♒ ☽✶♂ 0:50a ☽☌♅ 5:22p ☽△☿ 9:12p Raffi 1948 Jefferey Tambor 1944	**9** ☽v/c 3:28a ☽→♓ 5:05a ☽△♃ 3:28a ☽□♀ 2:21p Lisa Bates 1955 Dean Koontz 1945	**10** ☽ in ♓ ☽□♄ 1:23a ☽□♇ 7:28a ☽□♂ 12:51p ☽△☉ 7:14p Ron Glass 1945 Jerry Miller 1943	**11** ☽v/c 5:09p ☽→♈ 5:36p ☽□☿ 3:17p ☽□♃ 5:09p Stephen Lang 1952 Georgio Armani 1934	**12** ☽ in ♈ ☽✶♀ 8:44a ☽✶♆ 9:13a ♀△♆ 1:49p ☽✶♄ 2:01p ☿☌♃ 3:29p ☿→♋ 3:47p ♃→♋ 5:03p ☽△♇ 7:17p Buddy Foster 1957 Lisa Nicole Carson 1969	**13** ☽ in ♈ ☽v/c 4:52p Last Qtr. 21♈25 11:45a ☽△♂ 0:05a ☽□☉ 11:45a ☽✶♅ 4:52p Didi Conn 1951 Anders Jarryd 1961	**14** ☽→♉ 4:13a ☽✶♃ 4:51a ☽✶☿ 8:10a ☽□♆ 6:56p David Gordon 1936 Dale Robertson 1923
15 ☽ in ♉ ♀☌♄ 0:32a Joe Satriani 1956 Lolita Davidovich 1961	**16** ☽v/c 0:41a ☽→♊ 11:26a ☽✶☉ 0:23a ☽□♅ 0:41a Barnard Hughes 1915 Mary Baker Eddy 1821	**17** ☽ in ♊ ☽△♆ 1:03a ♀☍♇ 2:46a ☽⚻♄ 6:22a ☽☍♇ 9:58a ☽⚻♀ 10:37a ☽☍♂ 1:51p Regina Belle 1963 Erle Stanley Gardner 1887	**18** ☽v/c 4:46a ☽→♋ 2:56p ☽△♅ 4:46a ☽⚻♃ 5:08p Dion (DiMucci) 1939 Richard Branson 1950	**19** ☽ in ♋ ♀☍♂ 2:20a ☽⚻☿ 6:17a ♂SD 3:45p Campbell Scott 1962 Anthony Edwards 1962	**20** ☽v/c 12:44p ☽→♌ 3:43p New Moon 28♋08 12:44p ☽☌☉ 12:44p Paul Cook 1956 Stone Gossard 1966	**21** ☽ in ♌ ☽☍♆ 3:53a ☽✶♄ 9:36a ☽△♇ 12:08p ☽△♂ 3:49p ☽✶♀ 8:43p Patricia Elliot 1942 Emerson Hart 1969
22 ☽v/c 5:34a ☽→♍ 3:29p ☽☍♅ 5:34a ☉→♌ 11:26a ☽✶♃ 7:00p **Sun enters Leo** Emily Saliers 1963	**23** ☽ in ♍ ☽□♄ 9:48a ☽□♇ 12:00p ☽□♂ 3:56p ☽✶☿ 7:22p Haile Selassie 1891 Spencer Christian 1947	**24** ☽v/c 0:48a ☽→♎ 4:08p ☽□♀ 0:48a ☽✶☉ 7:51p ☽□♃ 8:32p Gus Van Sant 1952 Barry Lamar Bonds 1964	**25** ☽ in ♎ ☽△♆ 4:40a ☽△♄ 11:36a ☽✶♇ 1:30p ☽✶♂ 5:57p Jack Gilford 1913 Katherine Kelly Lang 1961	**26** ☽v/c 8:10a ☽→♏ 7:17p ☽□☿ 5:22a ☽△♀ 7:30a ☽△♅ 8:10a ♀△♅ 3:18p Dobie Gray 1942 Jeremy Piven 1965	**27** ☽ in ♏ First Qtr. 4♏27 3:08a ☽△♃ 0:46a ☽□☉ 3:08a ☽□♆ 8:30a Irv Cross 1939 Vincent Canby 1924	**28** ☽ in ♏ ☽v/c 8:50p ☽□♅ 1:45p ☽△☿ 8:50p Peter Duchin 1937 Elisabeth Berkeley 1972
29 ☽→♐ 1:44a LEO ☽△☉ 2:34p ☽✶♆ 3:40p Alexandra Paul 1963 Martina McBride 1966	**30** ☽ in ♐ ☽☍♄ 0:32a ☽☌♇ 1:45a ☿→♌ 3:18a ☉☍♆ 4:48a ☽☌♂ 7:54a ☽✶♅ 10:31p Ilene Kristen 1951 Lisa Kudrow 1963	**31** ☽v/c 9:24a ☽→♑ 11:16a ☽v/c 7:21p ☽☍♀ 9:24a ☽☍♃ 7:21p Kenny Burrell 1931 Evonne Goolagong Cawley '51				

JUNE 2001

S	M	T	W	T	F	S
					1	2
3	4	5	6	7	8	9
10	11	12	13	14	15	16
17	18	19	20	21	22	23
24	25	26	27	28	29	30

AUGUST 2001

S	M	T	W	T	F	S
			1	2	3	4
5	6	7	8	9	10	11
12	13	14	15	16	17	18
19	20	21	22	23	24	25
26	27	28	29	30	31	

Moon goes void-of-course.
Moon enters next sign.
☽v/c 12:44p
☽→♌ 3:43p
New Moon
28♋08
12:44p
☽☌☉ 12:44p
Paul Cook 1956
Stone Gossard 1966
Daily aspects (when exact).
Sign or Direction changes.

Pacific Daylight Saving Time

Day	☉	☿	♀	♂	♃	♄	♅	♆	♇	☊
1	10♌	05♌	01♋	16♐	04♊	12♊	23♒R	07♒R	13♐R	04♋R
2	11	07	02	17	05	12	23	07	13	04
3	12	08	03	17	05	13	23	07	13	04
4	13	10	04	18	05	13	23	07	13	04
5	14	12	05	18	05	13	23	07	13	04
6	15	14	06	18	06	13	23	07	13	04
7	16	16	07	19	06	13	23	07	13	04
8	17	18	09	20	06	13	23	07	13	04
9	18	20	10	20	06	13	23	07	13	04
10	18	22	11	21	06	13	23	07	13	04
11	19	24	12	21	07	13	23	07	13	04
12	20	26	13	22	07	13	23	07	13	03
13	21	28	14	22	07	13	23	07	13	03
14	22	30	16	23	07	14	23	07	13	03
15	23	01♍	16	23	07	14	23	07	13	03
16	24	03	17	24	08	14	23	07	13D	03
17	25	05	19	24	08	14	23	07	13	03
18	26	06	20	25	08	14	22	07	13	03
19	27	08	22	25	09	14	22	07	13	03
20	28	09	23	26	09	14	22	07	13	03
21	29	11	24	26	09	14	22	07	13	03
22	00♍	12	01♌	27	09	14	22	07	13	03
23	01	14	03	27	10	14	22	07	13	03
24	02	16	04	28	10	14	22	07	13	03
25	03	18	05	28	10	14	22	07	13	03
26	04	24	06	24	11	14	22	07	13	03
27	05	24	08	24	11	14	22	07	13	03
28	06	25	09	25	11	14	22	07	13	03
29	07	27	10	25	12	14	22	07	13	03
30	08	28	11	26	12	14	22	07	13	03
31	09	30	13	26	14	14	22	07	13	03

Above are rounded to nearest whole degree. Positions more than 29°30' round to 30° of one sign before 00' of the next sign. See pages 46-57 for a complete ephemeris.

AUGUST PLANTING DAYS
Above-ground crops: Best days: 23, 24 Good: 1, 2, 21, 22, 28, 29
Root crops/perennials: Best days: 5, 6, 7, 15, 16 Good : 10, 11, 12

PLANETS VISIBLE IN THE MORNING SKY
Venus, Jupiter, and Saturn. **Do not confuse** Venus with Jupiter
the first half of the month. Venus is brighter than Jupiter.
PLANETS VISIBLE IN THE EVENING SKY
Mercury beginning the 15th, Mars.

LEO ♌ July 22 to August 22 "I WILL"

A fixed, fire sign of positive polarity.
SYMBOL: the majestic lion.
RULING PLANET: the Sun.
KEYWORDS: leadership, generous, creative, dramatic, enthusiastic.

COLORS: gold and scarlet.
RULES: the heart and spine.

AUGUST

SUNDAY	MONDAY	TUESDAY	WEDNESDAY	THURSDAY	FRIDAY	SATURDAY
		JULY 2001 S M T W T F S 1 2 3 4 5 6 7 8 9 10 11 12 13 14 15 16 17 18 19 20 21 22 23 24 25 26 27 28 29 30 31 **SEPTEMBER 2001** S M T W T F S 1 2 3 4 5 6 7 8 9 10 11 12 13 14 15 16 17 18 19 20 21 22 23 24 25 26 27 28 29 30	**1** LEO ☽v/c in ♑ ♀→♋ 5:18a Taylor Fry 1981 Robert Cray 1953	**2** ☽→♒ 10:53p ☿☍♆ 2:58p Kathryn Harrod 1950 Carroll O'Connor 1924	Full Moon 11♒56 10:56p ☽ in ♒ ☽☌♆ 1:31p ☽☍☿ 6:23p ☽☍☉ 10:56p Ray Bloch 1902 Beverly Lee 1941	**4** ☽ in ♒ ☽v/c 9:52p ☽△♄ 0:05a ☽✶♇ 0:21a ☽✶♂ 8:45a ☉✶♄ 2:33p ☉△♇ 4:31p ☽☌♅ 9:52p Kenneth Dryden 1947 Billy Bob Thornton 1955
5 ☽→♓ 11:30a ☿✶♄ 4:11a ☿△♇ 4:27a ♄☍♇ 10:03a ☉☌☿ 2:51p ♀☌♃ 3:50p ☽△♃ 9:58p ☽△♀ 10:30p Sammi Smith 1943 Tawney Kitaen 1961	**6** ☽ in ♓ ☽v/c 10:39p ☽□♇ 1:02p ☽□♄ 1:15p ☽□♂ 10:39p Geri Halliwell 1973 Randy DeBarge 1958	**7** ☽v/c in ♓ ☿△♂ 1:38p Kate McNeil 1958 David Duchovny 1960	**8** ☽→♈ 0:05a ☽□♃ 11:27a ☽✶♆ 2:21p ☽□♀ 5:24p The Edge 1961 Nina Talbot 1930	**9** ☽ in ♈ ☽v/c 9:53p ☽△♇ 1:13a ☽✶♄ 1:52a ☽△☉ 10:17a ☽△♂ 11:56a ☽△☿ 7:54p ☽✶♅ 9:53p David Steinberg 1942 John R. Cappelletti 1952	**10** ☽→♉ 11:23a ☿☍♅ 7:58a ☉△♂ 2:46p ☽✶♃ 11:17p Neneh Cherry 1964 Noah Beery, Jr. 1913	**11** ☽ in ♉ ☽□♆ 1:01a ☽✶♀ 10:02a Chris Kelly 1978 Charlie Sexton 1968
Last Qtr. 19♉41 0:53a ☽v/c 3:32p ☽→♊ 7:59p ☽□☉ 0:53a ☽□♅ 7:02a ☽□☿ 3:32p **Perseids Meteors** Jennifer Warren 1941	**13** ☽ in ♊ ☽△♆ 8:41a ☽☍♇ 6:36p ☽●♄ 7:53p ☿→♍ 10:04p Joycelyn Elders 1933 Danny Bonaduce 1959	**14** ☽ in ♊ ☽v/c 12:42p ☽☍♂ 6:38a ☽✶☉ 11:11a ☽△♅ 12:42p David Crosby 1941 James Horner 1953	**15** ☽→♋ 0:55a ☽✶☿ 5:01a ☉☍♅ 8:25a ☽●♃ 12:50p Bobby Byrd 1934 Abby Dalton 1935	**16** ☽ in ♋ ☽v/c 6:03a ☽☌♀ 6:03a Laura Innes 1959 Eydie Gorme 1932	**17** ☽→♌ 2:25a ☽☍♆ 1:27p ☽△♇ 10:24p ☿✶♃ 11:57p Belinda Carlisle 1958 Martha Coolidge 1946	New Moon 26♌12 7:55p ☽ in ♌ ☽v/c 7:55p ☽✶♄ 0:03a ☽△♂ 11:26a ☽☍♅ 2:27p ☽☌☉ 7:55p Mika Boorem 1988 Marge Schott 1928
19 ☽→♍ 1:53a ☽✶♃ 2:09p ☽☌☿ 6:39p ☽□♇ 9:35p ☽□♄ 11:26p Matthew Perry 1969 Kyra Sedgwick 1965	**20** ☽ in ♍ ☽v/c 1:21p ☽□♂ 11:48a ☽✶♀ 1:21p ☿□♇ 8:23p Al Roker 1954 John Hiatt 1952	**21** ☽→♎ 1:19a ☽△♆ 12:17p ☿□♄ 2:10p ☽□♃ 2:32p ☽✶♇ 9:39p ☽△♄ 11:47p Alicia Witt 1975 Joe Strummer 1952	**22** ☽ in ♎ ☽v/c 6:34p ☽✶♂ 1:53p ☽△♅ 2:16p ☉→♍ 6:27p ☽□♀ 6:34p **Sun enters Virgo** Henri Cartier-Bresson 1908	**23** ☽→♏ 2:50a ♂✶♅ 2:56a ☽✶☉ 3:27a ♇SD 9:06a ☽□♆ 2:26p ☽△♃ 5:36p Tex Williams 1917 Patricia McBride 1942	**24** ☽ in ♏ ☽✶☿ 11:24a ☽□♅ 6:17p John Bush 1963 David Freiberg 1938	First Qtr. 2♐40 12:55p ☽v/c 4:16a ☽→♐ 7:59a ☽△♀ 4:16a ☽□☉ 12:55p ☽✶♆ 8:24p Sean Connery 1930 Jo Dee Messina 1969
26 ☽ in ♐ ☽☌♇ 7:24a ☽☍♄ 10:21a ♀→♌ 9:12p Branford Marsalis 1960 **Women's Equality Day**	**27** ☽v/c 5:50a ☽→♑ 5:02p ☽✶♅ 2:14a ☽□☿ 3:19a ☽☌♂ 5:50a Alex Lifeson 1953 Paul Reubens 1952	**28** ☽ in ♑ ☽△☉ 3:12a ☿□♂ 5:42a ☽☍♃ 11:33a Rita Dove 1952 Roger Tory Peterson 1908	**29** VIRGO ☽ in ♑ ☽v/c 11:28p ☽△☿ 11:28p John McCain 1936 Deb Van Valkenburgh 1952	**30** ☽→♒ 4:48a ☽☍♀ 1:39p ☽☌♆ 6:05p Peggy Lipton 1947 Timothy Bottoms 1951	**31** ☽ in ♒ ☽✶♇ 6:11a ☽△♄ 9:49a ☿→♎ 5:37p Gina Schock 1957 William Saroyan 1908	Moon goes void-of-course. Moon enters next sign. ☽v/c 4:16a ☽→♐ 7:59a First Qtr. 2♐40 12:55p ☽△♀ 4:16a ☽□☉ 12:55p ☽✶♆ 8:24p Sean Connery 1930 Jo Dee Messina 1969 Daily aspects (when exact). Sign or Direction changes.

Pacific Daylight Saving Time

Day	☉	☿	♀	♂	♃	♄	♅	♆	♇	☊
	10♍	01♎	07♌	27♐	10♋	14Ⅱ	22 R ♒	07♒	13♐	03♋
1	10	01	07	27	10	14	22	07	13	03
2	11	03	09	28	11	14	22	06	13	03
3	12	04	11	28	11	14	22	06	13	03
4	13	06	12	29	11	15	22	06	13	03
5	14	07	13	29	11	15	22	06	13	02
6	15	09	15	00♑	11	15	22	06	13	02
7	16	11	16	00	11	15	22	06	13	02
8	17	12	17	01	12	15	22	06	13	02
9	18	14	19	01	12	15	22	06	13	02
10	19	15	20	02	12	15	22	06	13	02
11	20	17	21	02	12	15	22	06	13	02
12	21	19	22	03	13	15	22	06	13	02
13	22	21	24	03	13	15	21	06	13	02
14	23	22	25	04	13	15 R	21	06	13	02
15	24	24	26	04	13	15	21	06	13	02
16	24	26	27	05	13	15	21	06	13	02
17	25	27	29	05	13	15	21	06	13	02
18	26	29	00♍	06	14	15	21	06	13	01
19	27	01♍	01	06	14	15	21	06	13	01
20	28	03	02	07	14	15	21	06	13	01
21	29	05	04	07	14	15	21	06	13	01
22	30	06	05	08	14	15	21	06	13	01
23	01♎	08	06	08	14	15	21	06	13	01
24	01	10	07	09	14	15	21	06	13	01
25	02	12	09	10	14	15	21	06	13	01
26	03	14	10	11	14	15	21	06	13	01
27	04	05	11	11	14	15	21	06	13	01
28	05	06	12	12	14	15	21	06	13	01
29	06	07	14	13	14	15	21	06	13	01
30	08	08	12	14	14	15	21	06	13	01

Above are rounded to nearest whole degree. Positions more than 29°30′ round to 30° of one sign before 00′ of the next sign. See pages 46–57 for a complete ephemeris.

SEPTEMBER PLANTING DAYS

Above-ground crops
  Best days: 2, 20, 21, 29, 30. Good days: 18, 19, 24, 25
Root crops and perennials: Best days: 3, 11, 12, 13. Good: 7, 8

PLANETS VISIBLE IN THE MORNING SKY
  Venus, Jupiter, and Saturn.

PLANETS VISIBLE IN THE EVENING SKY
  Mercury and Mars.

VIRGO ♍ August 22 to September 22 "I ANALYZE"

A mutable, earth sign of negative polarity.
SYMBOL: a virgin with a shaft of wheat.
COLORS: gray and navy blue.   RULING PLANET: Mercury.
RULES the intestinal tract and powers of assimilation.
KEYWORDS: discriminating, critical, methodical, analytical, service.

SEPTEMBER

SUNDAY	MONDAY	TUESDAY	WEDNESDAY	THURSDAY	FRIDAY	SATURDAY
			AUGUST 2001 S M T W T F S 1 2 3 4 5 6 7 8 9 10 11 12 13 14 15 16 17 18 19 20 21 22 23 24 25 26 27 28 29 30 31 **OCTOBER 2001** S M T W T F S 1 2 3 4 5 6 7 8 9 10 11 12 13 14 15 16 17 18 19 20 21 22 23 24 25 26 27 28 29 30 31	Moon goes void-of-course. Moon enters next sign. ☽v/c 3:27a ☽→♎ 12:00p New Moon 24♍36 3:27a ☽☌⊙ 3:27a ☿△♅ 6:49p ☽□♂ 7:58p ☽△♆ 9:54p Malik Yoba 1967 Rita Rudner 1955 Daily aspects (when exact). Sign or Direction changes.		**1** ☽v/c 10:36a ☽→♓ 5:32p ☽☌♅ 1:44a ♀☍♆ 8:55a ☽⚹♂ 10:36a Archie Bell 1944 Ron O'Neal 1937
2 ☽ in ♓ Full Moon 10♓28 2:43p ⊙⚹♃ 8:16a ☽△♃ 2:16p ☽☍⊙ 2:43p ☽□♇ 6:56p ☽□♄ 10:45p Eric Dickerson 1960 Cleveland Amory 1917	**3** ☽ in ♓ No exact aspects **Labor Day** Tompall Glasser 1933	**4** ☽v/c 1:37a ☽→♈ 5:58a ☽□♂ 1:37a ☽☍☿ 5:26p ☽⚹♆ 6:53p ⊙□♇ 6:54p John Preston 1968 Damon Wayans 1960	**5** ☽ in ♈ ☽□♃ 3:13a ☽△♀ 4:04a ☿△♆ 5:51a ☽△♇ 7:02a ☽⚹♄ 10:57a Dennis Dugan 1946 Andrew Ducote 1986	**6** ☽v/c 3:31p ☽→♉ 5:18p ☽⚹♅ 1:40a ♀△♇ 10:05a ☽△♂ 3:31p ⊙□♄ 9:12p Jane Curtin 1947 Jeff Foxworthy 1958	**7** ☽ in ♉ ☽□♆ 5:47a ☽⚹♃ 2:42p ☽□♀ 9:02p ☽△⊙ 11:36p Julie Kavner 1951 Michael Feinstein 1956	**8** ☽ in ♉ ☽v/c 11:30a ♀⚹♄ 3:15a ♂→♑ 10:51a ☽□♅ 11:30a ☿□♃ 7:30p Alan Feinstein 1941 Harland Howard 1927
9 ☽→♊ 2:41a ☽△♆ 2:32p ☿⚹♇ 9:40p **Grandparents' Day** Phyllis Whitney 1903	**10** ☽ in ♊ ☽v/c 6:42p Last Qtr. 18♊08 11:59a ☽☍♇ 2:00a ☽△☿ 2:28a ☽●♄ 5:50a ☽⚹♀ 10:46a ☽□⊙ 11:59a ☽△♅ 6:42p Joe Perry 1950 Collin Firth 1960	**11** ☽→♋ 9:09a ☽☍♂ 11:56a ☿△♄ 3:06p Betsy Drake 1923 Jimmie Davis 1899	**12** ☽ in ♋ ☽v/c 8:16p ☽●♃ 5:32a ☽□☿ 12:32p ☽⚹⊙ 8:16p Rachel Ward 1957 Norwood Fisher 1965	**13** ☽→♌ 12:16p ☽☍♆ 10:36p Jean Smart 1959 Maurice Jarre 1924	**14** ☽ in ♌ ♀☍♅ 0:06a ☽△♇ 8:57a ☽⚹♄ 12:27p ☽⚹☿ 6:12p ☽☍♅ 11:29p Dan Cortese 1968 Jack Hawkins 1910	**15** ☽v/c 1:35a ☽→♍ 12:39p ☽☌♀ 1:35a ☽△♂ 6:48p Josh Charles 1971 Gaylord Perry 1938
16 ☽ in ♍ ☽⚹♃ 8:05a ☽□♇ 8:42a ☽□♄ 12:08p Carl Andre 1935 Jayne Brook 1962	**17** ☽v/c 3:27a ☽→♎ 12:00p New Moon 24♍36 3:27a ☽☌⊙ 3:27a ☿△♅ 6:49p ☽□♂ 7:58p ☽△♆ 9:54p Malik Yoba 1967 Rita Rudner 1955	**18** ☽ in ♎ ☽□♃ 8:02a ☽⚹♇ 8:17a ☽△♄ 11:48a ☽△♅ 10:37p **Rosh Hashana begins** Jada Pinkett Smith 1971	**19** ☽v/c 9:38a ☽→♏ 12:27p ☽☌☿ 0:40a ☽⚹♀ 9:38a ☽□♆ 10:48p ☽⚹♂ 10:49p William Golding 1911 Trisha Yearwood 1964	**20** ☽ in ♏ ☽△♃ 10:03a ♀→♍ 7:09p Crispin Glover 1964 Kristen Johnston 1967	**21** ☽v/c 2:09p ☽→♐ 4:02p ☽□♅ 1:04a ☽⚹⊙ 2:09p ☽□♀ 6:08p Don Felder 1947 Faber Birren 1900	**22** ☽ in ♐ ☽⚹♆ 3:10a ☽☌♇ 3:18p ⊙→♎ 4:05p ☽☍♄ 7:19p **Sun enters Libra** **Autumnal Equinox**
23 ☽v/c 5:32p ☽→♑ 11:48 ☽⚹♅ 7:31a ☽⚹☿ 5:32p **30** ☽ in ♓ ☽v/c 6:02a ☽⚹♂ 0:24a ☽□♇ 1:57a ☽△♃ 4:00a ☽□♄ 6:02a	**24** ☽ in ♑ First Qtr. 1♑24 2:31a ☽□⊙ 2:31a ☽△♀ 8:10a ☽☌♂ 5:15p Kevin Sorbo 1958 Gordon Clapp 1948	**25** ☽ in ♑ ☽☍♃ 1:56a Phil Rizzuto 1918 Anson Williams 1949	**26** ☽v/c 7:38a ☽→♒ 11:05a ☽□☿ 7:38a ♄SR 5:04p ☽△⊙ 7:15p ☽☌♆ 11:25p Bryan Ferry 1945 Christine Todd Whitman 1946	**27** ☽ in ♒ ☽⚹♇ 1:06p ☽△♄ 5:21p **Yom Kippur** Wilford Brimley 1934 Catherine Marshall 1914	**28** ☽v/c 10:27p ☽→♓ 11:50p ☽☌♅ 6:15a ⊙△♆ 9:11p ☽△☿ 10:27p Jeffrey Jones 1947 **American Indian Day**	**29** ☽ in ♓ ☽☍♀ 10:25p Mike Post 1944 Patricia Hodge 1946

VIRGO

LIBRA

Pacific Daylight Saving Time

Above are rounded to nearest whole degree. Positions more than 29°30' round to 30° of one sign before 00° of the next sign. See pages 46-57 for a complete ephemeris.

Day	☉	☿	♀	♂	♃	♄	♅	♆	♇	☊
1	09♎	30♍R	13♍	13♐	14♋	15♊R	21♒R	06♒R	13♐	01♋
2	10	30♍D	15	14	14	15	21	06	13	01
3	11	29	16	15	14	15	21	06	13	01
4	12	29	17	16	14	15	21	06	13	01
5	13	29	18	16	15	15	21	06	13	01
6	14	28	20	17	15	15	21	06	13	01
7	15	27	21	18	15	15	21	06	13	00
8	16	26	22	18	15	15	21	06	13	00
9	17	25	23	19	15	15	21	06	13	00
10	18	23	24	20	15	15	21	06	13	00
11	19	22	26	20	15	15	21	06	13	00
12	20	20	27	21	15	15	21	06D	13	00
13	21	19	28	21	15	15	21	06	13	00
14	22	17	29	22	15	14	21	06	13	00
15	23	16	01♎	22	16	14	21	06	14	00
16	24	15	02	23	16	14	21	06	14	00
17	25	14	03	24	16	14	21	06	14	00
18	26	14	04	24	16	14	21	06	14	30♊
19	27	14D	06	25	16	14	21	06	14	30
20	28	15	07	25	16	14	21	06	14	30
21	29	17	08	26	16	14	21R	06	14	30
22	00♏	18	09	27	16	14	21	06	14	30
23	01♏	01♎	11	27	16	14	21	06	14	30
24	02	02	12	28	16	14	21	06	14	30
25	03	03	13	28	16	14	21	06	14	30
26	04	04	14	00♑	16	14	21	06	14	30
27	05	05	16	01	16	14	21	06	14	30
28	06	06	17	01	16	14	21	06	14	30
29	07	07	18	02	16	14	21	06	14	30
30	08	08	19	03	16	14	21D	06	14	30
31	09	09	20	03	16	14	21	06	14	30

OCTOBER PLANTING DAYS

Above-ground crops: Best days: 1, 17, 18, 26, 27, 28 Good: 21, 22, 23, 31
Root crops and perennials: Best days: 9, 10 Good days: 4, 5, 15, 16

PLANETS VISIBLE IN THE MORNING SKY
Mercury from 21st, Venus, Jupiter, and Saturn. **Do not confuse** Venus with Mercury from end of third week. Venus is brighter.
PLANETS VISIBLE IN THE EVENING SKY: Mercury to 8th, Mars.

LIBRA ♎ September 22 to October 23 "I BALANCE"

A cardinal, air sign of positive polarity.
SYMBOL: the balance (scales of justice), or the Sun on the horizon as the balance between night and day.
COLORS: lighter blues, pink and soft rose.
RULES the kidneys and lower back.   RULING PLANET: Venus.
KEYWORDS: balance, harmony, companionship, romance, negotiation.

OCTOBER

SUNDAY	MONDAY	TUESDAY	WEDNESDAY	THURSDAY	FRIDAY	SATURDAY
SEPTEMBER 2001 S M T W T F S 1 2 3 4 5 6 7 8 9 10 11 12 13 14 15 16 17 18 19 20 21 22 23 24 25 26 27 28 29 30 NOVEMBER 2001 S M T W T F S 1 2 3 4 5 6 7 8 9 10 11 12 13 14 15 16 17 18 19 20 21 22 23 24 25 26 27 28 29 30	**1** ☽→♈ 12:08p ♀□♇ 9:12a ♀△♂ 11:03a ☿SR 12:23p Walter Matthau 1920 Elizabeth Dennehy 1960	☽ in ♈ **Harvest Moon** Full Moon 9♈26 6:49a ☽✶♆ 0:09a ☽☍☉ 6:49a ♀✶♃ 8:49a ☽△♇ 1:48p ☽□♂ 3:22p ☽□♃ 4:11p ☽✶♄ 5:39p ♀□♄ 11:54p **Sukkoth** Phil Oakley 1955 Bud Graugh 1967	**3** ☽v/c 9:44p ☽→♉ 11:01p ☽✶♅ 5:56a ♂☍♃ 10:09a ☽☍☿ 9:44p Fred Couples 1959 Neve Campbell 1973	**4** ☽ in ♉ LIBRA ☽□♆ 10:41a John Secada 1961 Alan Rosenberg 1950	**5** ☽ in ♉ ☽v/c 3:33p ☽✶♃ 2:43a ☽△♂ 4:32a ☽△♀ 9:19a ☽□♅ 3:33p ☉✶♇ 11:00p Larry Fine 1911 Clive Barker 1952	**6** ☽→♊ 8:12a ☽△♆ 7:28p Jenny Lind 1820 Britt Ekland 1942
7 ☽ in ♊ ☽☍♇ 8:31a ☽△☉ 11:12a ☽●♄ 11:48a ☉□♃ 1:08p ☉△♄ 6:56p ☽□♀ 11:08p ☽△♅ 11:15p Judy Landers 1961 Christopher Norris 1953	**8** ☽v/c 9:24a ☽→♋ 3:19p ☽△☿ 9:24a **Columbus Day** **Thanksgiving (Canada)**	☽ in ♋ Last Qtr. 16♋56 9:20p ☽☌♃ 5:35p ☽□☉ 9:20p ☽☍♂ 11:55p Joe Pepitone 1940 Fyvush Finkel 1923	**10** ☽v/c 10:47a ☽→♌ 7:54p ☽✶♀ 9:43a ☽□☿ 10:47a Peter Coyote 1942 **Draconids Meteors**	**11** ☽ in ♌ ☽☍♆ 6:07a ☽△♇ 6:12p ☽✶♄ 8:49p Kyoko Ina 1972 Felton Perry 1946	**12** ☽v/c 9:34a ☽→♍ 9:58p ☽✶☉ 4:11a ☽☍♅ 7:15a ☽✶☿ 9:34a Sam Moore 1935 Richard Price 1949	**13** ☽ in ♍ ☿△♅ 1:45p ☿□♂ 5:36p ☉☌☿ 6:43p ☽□♇ 7:28p ☽□♄ 9:49p ☽✶♃ 10:26p Chris Carter 1957 Laraine Day 1920
14 ☽v/c 9:52p ☽→♎ 10:26p ☉△♅ 0:36a ☉□♂ 0:38a ☽△♂ 8:21a ☽☌♀ 9:52p Sheila Young 1950 Carroll Ballard 1937	**15** ☽ in ♎ ♀→♎ 4:42a ☽△♆ 8:05a ☽✶♇ 7:51p ☽△♄ 10:00p ☽□♃ 10:55p Jan Miner 1917 Don Stevenson 1942	☽v/c 12:23p ☽→♏ 11:02p New Moon 23♎30 12:23p ☽☌☿ 3:32a ☽△♅ 8:19a ☽□♂ 10:58a ☽☌☉ 12:23p Kelly Martin 1975 David Zucker 1947	**17** ☽ in ♏ ☽□♆ 8:57a ♆SD 6:49p Julie Adams 1926 Alan Jackson 1958	**18** ☽ in ♏ ☽v/c 3:30p ☽△♃ 0:33a ☽□♅ 10:10a ☽✶♂ 3:30p Keith Jackson 1928 Melina Mercouri 1925	**19** ☽→♐ 1:47a ☿□♃ 4:48a ☽✶♀ 11:05a ☽✶♆ 12:20p Charles Chase 1952 Adm. Arleigh A. Burke 1901	**20** ☽ in ♐ ♀△♆ 0:36a ☽☌♇ 1:36a ☽☍♄ 3:31a ☽✶☿ 4:08a ☽✶♅ 3:21p **Sweetest's Day** Keith Hernandez 1953
21 ☽v/c 4:42a ☽→♑ 8:11a ☿△♄ 3:45a ☽✶☉ 4:42a **Orionids Meteors** Everett McGill 1953	**22** ☽ in ♑ ☽□♀ 0:16a ☽□☿ 11:21a ☽☍♃ 1:52p ☿SD 5:23p Derek Jacobi 1938 Curly Howard 1903	☽v/c 1:12p ☽→♒ 6:26p First Qtr. 0♒46 7:58p ☉→♏ 1:26a ☽●♂ 1:12p ☿△♄ 7:42p ☽□☉ 7:58p Brooke Theiss 1969 **Sun enters Scorpio**	**24** ☽ in ♒ ☽☌♆ 6:27a ☽△♀ 6:16p ☽✶♇ 9:39p ☽△♄ 11:03p ☽△☿ 11:53p Y.A. Tittle 1926 **United Nations Day**	**25** ☽ in ♒ ☽v/c 12:32p ☽☌♅ 12:32p Kornelia Ender 1958 John Matuszak 1950	**26** ☽→♓ 6:56a ♀✶♇ 3:19a ☽△☉ 2:03p ♀△♄ 2:24p ☿□♃ 5:55p Bob Hoskins 1942 Keith Strickland 1953	**27** ☽ in ♓ ☽v/c 2:31p ♂→♒ 10:19a ☽□♇ 10:30a ☽□♄ 11:29a ☽△♃ 2:31p ♀□♃ 6:36p Peter Firth 1953 Jayne Kennedy-Overton '51
28 ☽→♈ 6:15p ☽✶♂ 8:14p Dennis Franz 1944 **Daylight Saving Time ends**	**29** ☽ in ♈ ☉□♆ 1:31a ☽✶♆ 6:12a ☽△♇ 9:17p ☽✶♄ 9:50p Nia Long 1970 Yasmin LeBon 1964	**30** ☽ in ♈ ☽v/c 11:17a ☽□♃ 1:06a ☽☍♀ 7:17a ☽☍☿ 7:19a ☿☌♀ 10:54a ☽✶♅ 11:17a ♅SD 2:55p Eddie Holland 1939 Timothy B. Schmit 1947	☽→♉ 4:48a **Blue Moon** Full Moon 8♉52 9:41p ☽□♂ 10:06a ☽□♆ 4:20p ☽☍☉ 9:41p ♀△♅ 10:59p **Halloween** Lee Grant 1926 Dermot Mulroney 1963	OCTOBER		Moon goes void-of-course. Moon enters next sign. ☽v/c 1:12p ☽→♒ 6:26p First Qtr. 0♒46 7:58p ☉→♏ 1:26a ☽●♂ 1:12p ☿△♄ 7:42p ☽□☉ 7:58p Brooke Theiss 1969 Sun enters Scorpio Daily aspects (when exact). Sign or Direction changes.

Pacific Daylight Saving Time ends at 2:00am October 28th. **Turn clocks back one hour.**

Above are rounded to nearest whole degree. Positions more than 29°30' round to 30° / of one sign before 00° of the next sign. See pages 46-57 for a complete ephemeris.

Day	☉	☿	♀	♂	♃	♄	♅	♆	♇	☊
1	10♏	22♏	22♏	04♒	16♋R	14♊R	21♒	06♒	14♐	30♊
2	11	23	23	04	16R	14R	21	06	14	29
3	12	24	24	05	16	14	21	06	14	29
4	13	26	26	06	16	14	21	06	14	29
5	14	27	27	07	16	14	21	06	14	29
6	15	00♐	00♏	08	16	14	21	06	14	29
7	16	01	01	09	16	13	21	06	14	29
8	17	02	03	10	16	13	21	06	14	29
9	18	03	03	11	16	13	21	06	14	29
10	19	05	04	12	16	13	21	06	14	29
11	20	06	06	13	16	13	21	06	14	29
12	21	08	07	14	15	13	21	06	14	29
13	22	09	08	15	15	13	21	06	14	29
14	23	11	09	16	15	13	20	06	14	28
15	24	12	11	17	15	13	20	06	15	28
16	25	14	12	18	15	13	20	06	15	28
17	26	15	12	19	15	13	20	06	15	28
18	27	17	13	20	15	12	20	06	15	28
19	28	18	14	21	15	12	20	06	15	28
20	29	20	16	22	15	12	20	06	15	28
21	00♐	21	17	23	15	12	20	06	15	28
22	01♐	23	18	23	14	12	20	07	15	28
23	02	24	19	24	14	12	20	07	15	28
24	03	26	21	25	14	12	20	07	15	28
25	04	27	22	26	14	12	20	07	15	28
26	05	00♐	23	26	14	12	20	07	15	28
27	06	02	24	27	14	12	20	07	15	28
28	07	03	26	28	14	12	20	07	15	28
29	08	05	27	28	14	12	20	07	15	28
30	09	07	28	29	14	12	20	07	15	28

NOVEMBER PLANTING DAYS

Above-ground crops: Best days: 23, 24   Good days: 18, 19, 28, 29
Root crops & perennials: Best days: 5, 6, 13, 14   Good: 1, 2, 11, 12

PLANETS VISIBLE IN THE MORNING SKY
Mercury to the 18th. Venus, Jupiter, and Saturn. **Do not confuse**
Venus with Mercury the first half of the month. Venus is brighter.
PLANET VISIBLE IN THE EVENING SKY
Mars.

SCORPIO ♏   October 23 to November 21/22   "I CREATE"

A fixed, water sign of negative polarity.
SYMBOLS: the scorpion, eagle, and phoenix, the mythical bird con-
sumed by the fire of the Sun which arose again from its own ashes.
COLORS: deep reds.   RULES the generative system.
RULING PLANETS: Mars and Pluto.
KEYWORDS: resourceful, secretive, passionate, intense, transformative.

NOVEMBER

S	M	T	W	T	F	S
			OCTOBER 2001 S M T W T F S 1 2 3 4 5 6 7 8 9 10 11 12 13 14 15 16 17 18 19 20 21 22 23 24 25 26 27 28 29 30 31 DECEMBER 2001 S M T W T F S 1 2 3 4 5 6 7 8 9 10 11 12 13 14 15 16 17 18 19 20 21 22 23 24 25 26 27 28 29 30 31	**1** ☽ in ♉ ☽v/c 8:20p ☿△♅ 1:04a ☽✶♃ 10:33a ☽□♅ 8:20p ♄☍♇ 10:08p **All Saints' Day** Jeannie Berlin 1949	**2** ☽→♊ 1:12p ♃SR 7:35a ☽△♂ 9:28p ☿☌♀ 11:28p Charlie Walker 1926 Earl "Speedo" Carroll 1937	**3** ☽ in ♊ ☽△♆ 0:23a ☽☌♄ 2:21p ☽☍♇ 2:39p John Barry 1933 Shadoe Stevens 1946
4 ☽v/c 11:45a ☽→♋ 7:44p ☽△♅ 3:24a ☽△♀ 11:18a ☽△☿ 11:45a Van Stephenson 1953 Matthew McConaughey '69	**5** ☽ in ♋ ♂☌♆ 4:44a ☽△☉ 8:16p ☽☌♃ 11:32p Corin Nemec 1971 Scott Steeplton 1962	**6** ☽ in ♋ ☽v/c 11:10p ☽□♀ 9:41p ☽□☿ 11:10p **Election Day** Francis Lederer 1906	**7** ☽→♌ 0:34a ☽☍♆ 11:08a ☿→♏ 11:53a ☽☍♂ 1:58p ☉△♃ 4:01p ☽✶♄ 11:42p Dean Jagger 1903 Barry Newman 1938	**8** ☽ in ♌ ☽v/c 12:30p Last Qtr. 16♌10 4:21a ☽△♇ 0:43a ☽□☉ 4:21a ♀→♏ 5:28a ☽☍♅ 12:30p Esther Rolle 1933 Christiaan Barnard 1922	**9** ☽→♍ 3:49a ☽✶♀ 5:58a ☽✶☿ 8:39a Billie August 1948 Bob Graham 1936	**10** ☽ in ♍ ☽v/c 10:40a ☽□♄ 2:05a ☽□♇ 3:27a ☽✶♃ 5:55a ☽✶☉ 10:40a Alaina Reed-Hall 1946 Ronald Emmerich 1955
11 ☽→♎ 5:53a ☿□♆ 10:59a ☽△♆ 4:07p ☽△♂ 11:54p **Veterans' Day** Calista Flockhart 1964	**12** ☽ in ♎ ☽v/c 4:41p ☽△♄ 3:40a ☽✶♇ 5:23a ☽□♃ 7:37a ☽△♅ 4:41p ☉□♅ 11:32p Jimmy Hayes 1943 David Ellefson 1964	**13** ☽→♏ 7:44a ♀□♆ 4:02a ☽□♆ 6:09p ☽☌♀ 7:29p Walter Kibby 1964 Ray Wylie Hubbard 1946	**14** ☽ in ♏ ☽v/c 10:40p New Moon 22♏58 10:40p ☽☌☿ 1:01a ☽□♂ 4:40a ☽△♃ 9:48a ☽□♅ 7:18p ♂△♄ 10:00p ☽☌☉ 10:40p P. J. O'Rourke 1947 Buckwheat Zydeco 1947	**15** ☽→♐ 10:51a *get Calendars for year 2002* ☽✶♆ 9:46p Joanna Barnes 1934 Joseph Wapner 1919	**16** ☽ in ♐ ☿□♂ 8:33a ☽☍♄ 9:27a ☽✶♂ 11:39a ☽☌♇ 12:09p ♂✶♇ 9:26p Bryan Adams 1969 Joanna Pettet 1944	**17** ☽v/c 0:14a ☽→♑ 4:40p ☽✶♅ 0:14a ☿△♃ 4:57a **Sadie Hawkins' Day** **Leonids meteor showers**
18 ☽ in ♑ ☽✶♀ 5:21p ☽☍♃ 9:18p Brenda Vaccaro 1939 Andrea Marcovicci 1948	**19** ☽ in ♑ ☽v/c 9:57p ☽✶☿ 3:24a ☽✶☉ 9:57p Meg Ryan 1961 Glynnis O'Connor 1955	**20** ☽→♒ 1:55a ♀△♃ 7:31a ☽☌♆ 2:22p ☿□♅ 7:51p Beryl Sprinkel 1923 Richard Masur 1948	**21** ☽ in ♒ ☽v/c 11:37p ☽△♄ 2:36a ☽✶♇ 6:41a ☽□♀ 10:50a ☽☌♂ 1:01p ☽☌♅ 7:57p ☉→♐ 10:01p ☽□☿ 11:37p Bjork 1965 Juliet Mills 1941 **Sun enters Sagittarius**	**22** ☽→♓ 1:52p First Qtr. 0♓44 3:21p ☽□☉ 3:21p Patra 1972 **Thanksgiving Day**	**23** ☽ in ♓ ♀□♂ 8:43a ☽□♄ 2:41p ☽□♇ 7:24p ☽△♃ 8:03p Sam Keen 1931 Michael Wayne 1934	**24** ☽ in ♓ ☽v/c 9:29p ☽△♀ 6:32a ☽△☿ 9:29p Lisa Howard 1963 Claudia Dreifus 1944
25 ☽→♈ 2:21a ♀□♅ 2:50a ☽△☉ 9:21a ☽✶♆ 3:07p Etta Jones 1928 Percy Sledge 1940	**26** ☽ in ♈ ☽v/c 8:43p ☽✶♄ 2:17a ☽△♇ 7:27a ☽□♃ 7:32a ☿→♐ 10:24a ♂☌♅ 11:07a ☽✶♅ 8:11p ☽✶♂ 8:43p Marian Mercer 1935 Eugene Ionesco 1912	**27** ☽→♉ 1:06p No exact aspects James Avery 1948 Charlie Burchill 1959	**28** ☽ in ♉ ☽□♆ 1:24a ☉✶♆ 7:35a ☽✶♃ 4:35p Nancy Mitford 1904 S. Epatha Merkerson 1952	**29** ☽v/c 3:21p ☽→♊ 9:04p ☽□♅ 5:05a ☽□♂ 8:50a ☽☍♀ 3:21p Paul Simon 1928 Cathy Moriarty 1960	**30** ☽ in ♊ Full Moon 8♊43 12:49p ☽☍☿ 8:14a ☽△♆ 8:52a ☽☍☉ 12:49p ☿✶♆ 1:40p ☽☌♄ 6:08p ☽☍♇ 11:50p June Pointer 1954 Shirley Chisholm 1924	Moon goes void-of-course. Moon enters next sign. ☽v/c 11:37a ☽→♓ 1:52p First Qtr. 0♓44 3:21p ☽□☿ 11:37a ☽□☉ 3:21p Patra 1972 **Thanksgiving Day** Daily aspects (when exact). Sign or Direction changes.

SAGITTARIUS

Pacific Standard Time

Day	☉	☿	♀	♂	♃ R	♄ R	♅	♆	♇	☊
1	10♐	08♐	29♏	25♏	14♊	12♊	21♒	07♒	15♐	28♊
2	11	09	01♐	26	14	11	21	07	15	28
3	12	11	02	27	14	11	21	07	15	28
4	13	12	03	28	14	11	21	07	15	28
5	14	14	04	29	14	11	21	07	15	28
6	15	15	06	00♐	14	11	21	07	15	28
7	16	17	07	01	14	11	21	07	15	28
8	17	19	08	02	14	10	22	07	15	28
9	18	21	09	03	13	10	22	07	15	28
10	19	22	11	04	13	10	22	07	15	27
11	20	24	12	05	13	10	22	07	15	27
12	21	26	13	06	13	10	22	07	15	27
13	22	28	15	07	13	10	22	07	16	27
14	23	00♑	16	08	13	10	22	07	16	27
15	24	02	17	09	13	10	22	07	16	27
16	25	03	18	10	12	10	22	07	16	27
17	26	05	20	11	12	10	22	07	16	27
18	27	07	21	12	12	10	22	07	16	27
19	28	09	22	13	12	10	22	07	16	27
20	29	10	23	14	12	10	22	07	16	27
21	00♑	12	25	15	12	10	22	07	16	27
22	01	14	26	16	11	10	22	07	16	27
23	02	15	27	17	11	10	22	07	16	27
24	03	17	29	18	11	09	22	07	16	27
25	04	19	00♑	19	11	09	22	07	16	26
26	05	21	01	20	11	09	22	07	16	26
27	06	22	03	21	11	09	22	07	16	26
28	07	24	04	22	11	09	22	07	16	26
29	08	26	05	23	11	09	22	07	16	26
30	09	27	06	16♑	11	09	22	07	16	26
31	10	07	07	17	11	09	22	07	16	26

Above are rounded to nearest whole degree. Positions more than 29°30' round to 30° of one sign before 00° of the next sign. See pages 46-57 for a complete ephemeris.

DECEMBER PLANTING DAYS
Above-ground crops: Best days: 20, 21, 29   Good: 15, 16, 25, 26
Root crops/perennials: Best days: 2, 3, 11, 12, 30, 31   Good: 8, 9, 10

PLANETS VISIBLE IN THE MORNING SKY
Venus to the 3rd, Jupiter, and Saturn to the 3rd.
PLANETS VISIBLE IN THE EVENING SKY
Mercury beginning the 21st, Mars, and Saturn beginning the 3rd.

SAGITTARIUS ♐ November 21/22 to December 21   "I PERCEIVE"
A mutable, fire sign of positive polarity.
SYMBOL: the centaur.   COLORS: purple and deep blue.
RULING PLANET: Jupiter.   RULES: the hips and thighs.

SAGITTARIUS

DECEMBER

			NOVEMBER 2001 S M T W T F S 1 2 3 4 5 6 7 8 9 10 11 12 13 14 15 16 17 18 19 20 21 22 23 24 25 26 27 28 29 30 **JANUARY 2002** S M T W T F S 1 2 3 4 5 6 7 8 9 10 11 12 13 14 15 16 17 18 19 20 21 22 23 24 25 26 27 28 29 30 31	Moon goes void-of-course. Moon enters next sign. ☽v/c 0:44a ☽→♈ 10:45a First Qtr. 1♈05 12:56p ☽□♀ 0:44a ♂□♄ 5:35a ☽□☉ 12:56p ☿☍♃ 10:59p Hector Elizondo 1936 Andre Kostelanetz 1901 Daily aspects (when exact). Sign or Direction changes.		**1** ☽ in ♊ ☽v/c 5:48p ☽△♅ 11:17a ☽△♂ 5:48p John Densmore 1944 Robert Symonds 1926
2 ☽→♋ 2:30a ♀→♐ 3:12a **Advent begins** Rena Sofer 1968	**3** ☽ in ♋ ☽v/c 3:04a ☽☌♃ 3:04a ☉☍♄ 6:13a ☿☍♄ 4:47p Daryl Hannah 1961 Brendan Fraser 1968	**4** ☽→♌ 6:15a ☽△♀ 11:16a ☉☌☿ 1:36p ☽☍♆ 5:33p Cassandra Wilson 1955 "Moby Grape" Mosely 1942	**5** ☽ in ♌ ☽✶♄ 1:33a ☽△☉ 5:10a ☽△☿ 5:52a ☽△♇ 7:51a ☽☍♅ 6:43p Calvin Trillin 1935 John Rzeznick 1965	**6** ☽v/c 6:20a ☽→♍ 9:11a ☿☌♇ 0:12a ☽☍♂ 6:20a ☽□♀ 7:06p ☉☌♇ 7:53p Len Barry 1942 Alfred Eisenstaedt 1898	Last Qtr. 15♍47 11:52a **7** ☽ in ♍ ☽v/c 2:57p ☽□♄ 4:03a ☽✶♃ 8:23a ☽□♇ 10:45a ♀✶♆ 10:59a ☽□☉ 11:52a ☽□☿ 2:57p Edd Hall 1958 Ted Knight 1923	**8** ☽→♎ 11:57a ♂→♓ 1:52p ☽△♆ 11:23p Malcolm Gets 1963 David Carradine 1936
9 ☽ in ♎ ☽✶♀ 2:52a ☽△♄ 6:37a ☽□♃ 10:53a ☽✶♇ 1:48p ☽✶☉ 6:45p Joe Lando 1961 Joan Armatrading 1950	**10** ☽v/c 0:43a ☽→♏ 3:09p ☽✶☿ 0:19a ☽△♅ 0:43a ☿✶♅ 3:56a ☽△♂ 5:52p ♀☍♄ 6:33p **Hanukkah** Tommy Kirk 1941 Nia Peeples 1961	**11** ☽ in ♏ ☽□♆ 2:53a ☽△♃ 2:05p Christina Onassis 1950 Jermaine Jackson 1954	**12** ☽v/c 4:48a ☽→♐ 7:30p ☽□♅ 4:48a Bob Pettit 1932 Mike Pinder 1942	**13** ☽ in ♐ ☽□♂ 1:18a ☽✶♆ 7:43a ☉✶♅ 7:49a ☽☍♄ 2:29p ☽☌♀ 10:02p ☽☌♇ 11:02p **Geminids Meteors** Robert Prosky 1930	**14** **Solar Eclipse** New Moon 22♐56 12:47p ☽ in ♐ ♀☌♇ 8:50a ☽✶♅ 10:37a ☽●☉ 12:47p Dee Wallace Stone 1949 Stanley Roger Smith 1946	**15** ☽v/c 0:24a ☽→♑ 1:48a ☽☌☿ 0:24a ☽✶♂ 11:08a ☿→♑ 11:55a Don Franklin 1960 Don Johnson 1949
16 ☽ in ♑ ☽v/c 1:35a ☽☍♃ 1:35a Joyce Bulifant 1937 Benjamin Bratt 1963	**17** ☽→♒ 10:43a No exact aspects Bill Pullman 1954 Milla Jovovich 1975	**18** ☽ in ♒ ☽☌♆ 0:23a ☽△♄ 6:49a ☽✶♇ 5:17p Tracy Byrd 1966 Gillian Armstrong 1950	**19** ☽v/c 6:41p ☽→♓ 10:09p ☽✶♀ 5:05a ☽☌♅ 5:58a ♀✶♅ 1:41p ☽✶☉ 6:41p Cicely Tyson 1939 James Booth 1930	**20** ☽ in ♓ ☽✶☿ 2:28p ☽☌♂ 3:58p ☽□♄ 6:30p ☽△♃ 10:35p John Hillerman 1932 Chris Robinson 1966	**21** ☽ in ♓ ☽□♇ 5:46a ☿✶♂ 9:48a ☉→♑ 11:22a **Winter Solstice** **Sun enters Capricorn**	**22** First Qtr. 1♈05 12:56p ☽v/c 0:44a ☽→♈ 10:45a ☽□♀ 0:44a ♂□♄ 5:35a ☽□☉ 12:56p ☿☍♃ 10:59p Hector Elizondo 1936 Andre Kostelanetz 1901
23 ☽ in ♈ ☽✶♆ 1:08a ☽✶♄ 6:37a ☽□♃ 10:21a ☽□☿ 12:13p ☽△♇ 6:15p	**24** ☽v/c 7:21p ☽→♉ 10:12p ☽✶♅ 6:51a ♂△♃ 11:54a ☽△♀ 7:21p	**25** ☽ in ♉ ☽△☉ 5:36a ☽□♆ 12:09p ☽✶♃ 8:10p ☽✶♂ 10:30p ♀→♑ 11:25p **Christmas** Little Richard 1935 Robin Campbell 1954	**26** ☽ in ♉ ☽v/c 4:22p ☽△☿ 6:51a ☽□♅ 4:22p John Walsh 1943 Elisha Cook, Jr. 1913	**27** ☽→♊ 6:39a ☽△♆ 7:53p ☽●♄ 11:54p Wilson Cruz 1973 James McClure 1904	**28** ☽ in ♊ ☽v/c 10:24p ☽□♂ 8:36a ☽☍♇ 11:10a ☽△♅ 10:24p Joe Diffie 1958 Kary Bank Mullis 1945	**29** ☽→♋ 11:40a ☽☍♀ 7:58p Jason Gould 1966 Viveca Lindfors 1920
30 ☽ in ♋ ☽●☉ 2:40a ☽●♃ 6:09a ♂□♇ 10:50a ☽△♂ 3:01p **Lunar Eclipse** Full Moon 8♋48 2:40a	**31** ☽v/c 5:43a ☽→♌ 2:09p ☽☍☿ 5:43a ☉☍♃ 9:53p					

SAGITTARIUS

Pacific Standard Time

JANUARY 2001 — Noon Greenwich Mean Time

Day	☉	☽	☿	♀	♂	♃	♄	♅	♆	♇
1	11♑08 31	24♓46 01	15♑05	27♒31	5♏14	2R09	24R34	18♒40	5♒21	13♐47
2	12 09 41	7♈05 50	16 43	28 37	5 49	2♌04	24♉32	18 43	5 23	13 49
3	13 10 50	19 44 32	18 21	29 43	6 24	2 00	24 29	18 46	5 25	13 51
4	14 11 59	2♉46 08	19 59	0♓48	6 59	1 56	24 27	18 49	5 27	13 53
5	15 13 08	16 13 45	21 37	1 54	7 34	1 52	24 25	18 52	5 29	13 55
6	16 14 16	0♊08 55	23 16	2 59	8 08	1 48	24 23	18 55	5 32	13 57
7	17 15 24	14 30 59	24 55	4 03	8 43	1 44	24 21	18 58	5 34	13 59
8	18 16 32	29 16 35	26 35	5 08	9 18	1 40	24 19	19 02	5 36	14 01
9	19 17 40	14♋19 54	28 14	6 12	9 53	1 37	24 17	19 05	5 38	14 03
10	20 18 47	29 31 28	29 54	7 16	10 27	1 34	24 15	19 08	5 40	14 05
11	21 19 54	14♌52 43	1♒34	8 19	11 02	1 31	24 14	19 11	5 43	14 07
12	22 21 00	29 43 30	3 14	9 22	11 36	1 28	24 12	19 14	5 45	14 09
13	23 22 07	14♍26 22	4 53	10 25	12 11	1 26	24 11	19 17	5 47	14 11
14	24 23 13	28 45 53	6 33	11 27	12 45	1 23	24 10	19 21	5 49	14 13
15	25 24 19	12♎39 32	8 12	12 29	13 19	1 21	24 09	19 24	5 52	14 15
16	26 25 25	26 07 16	9 51	13 31	13 53	1 19	24 08	19 27	5 54	14 17
17	27 26 31	9♏10 56	11 29	14 32	14 28	1 18	24 07	19 30	5 56	14 19
18	28 27 37	21 53 34	13 06	15 33	15 02	1 16	24 06	19 34	5 58	14 21
19	29 28 42	4♐18 47	14 42	16 33	15 36	1 15	24 05	19 37	6 01	14 22
20	0♒29 47	16 30 16	16 17	17 33	16 10	1 14	24 05	19 40	6 03	14 24
21	1 30 52	28 31 33	17 50	18 33	16 44	1 13	24 04	19 44	6 05	14 26
22	2 31 56	10♑25 47	19 20	19 32	17 17	1 12	24 04	19 47	6 07	14 28
23	3 32 59	22 15 39	20 48	20 30	17 51	1 12	24 04	19 50	6 10	14 29
24	4 34 02	4♒03 33	22 12	21 28	18 25	1 11	24 04	19 54	6 12	14 31
25	5 35 03	15 51 34	23 33	22 26	18 58	1 11	24 04	19 57	6 14	14 33
26	6 36 04	27 41 41	24 49	23 23	19 32	1 11	24 04	20 01	6 17	14 34
27	7 37 04	9♓35 55	25 59	24 19	20 05	1 12	24 04	20 04	6 19	14 36
28	8 38 03	21 36 33	27 04	25 15	20 38	1 12	24 05	20 07	6 21	14 37
29	9 39 01	3♈46 07	28 02	26 10	21 11	1 13	24 05	20 11	6 23	14 39
30	10 39 57	16 07 36	28 52	27 05	21 45	1 14	24 05	20 14	6 26	14 40
31	11 40 53	28 44 16	29 33	27 59	22 18	1 15	24 06	20 18	6 28	14 42

Day	Sidereal Time	☽ Node	☉	☽	☿	♀	♂	♃	♄	♅	♆	♇
	H M S	° '	° '	° '	° '	° '	° '	° '	° '	° '	° '	° '
1	18:44:50	15♋39	22S58	6S38	24S34	13S44	12S05	19N48	16N47	15S53	18S46	12S12
3	18:52:43	15 33	22 47	2N49	24 14	12 51	12 28	19 47	16 46	15 51	18 45	12 13
5	19:00:36	15 27	22 34	12 19	23 47	11 56	12 51	19 46	16 46	15 49	18 44	12 13
7	19:08:29	15 20	22 19	19 49	23 14	11 01	13 14	19 44	16 45	15 47	18 43	12 13
9	19:16:22	15 14	22 03	23 32	22 35	10 06	13 39	19 44	16 45	15 45	18 42	12 14
11	19:24:15	15 08	21 45	18 54	21 50	9 09	13 58	19 43	16 45	15 43	18 41	12 14
13	19:32:08	15 01	21 26	10 19	20 59	8 12	14 20	19 42	16 44	15 41	18 40	12 14
15	19:40:02	14 55	21 03	0S08	20 02	7 15	14 41	19 42	16 44	15 39	18 39	12 14
17	19:47:55	14 49	20 40	9 57	18 59	6 17	15 02	19 42	16 44	15 37	18 38	12 14
19	19:55:48	14 42	20 16	17 34	17 52	5 19	15 22	19 42	16 45	15 35	18 36	12 14
21	20:03:41	14 36	19 49	21 53	16 40	4 21	15 42	19 42	16 45	15 33	18 35	12 14
23	20:11:34	14 30	19 22	22 13	15 26	3 22	16 02	19 42	16 45	15 31	18 34	12 14
25	20:19:27	14 23	18 52	18 37	14 11	2 24	16 21	19 42	16 46	15 28	18 33	12 14
27	20:27:20	14 17	18 22	11 55	12 58	1 27	16 39	19 43	16 46	15 26	18 32	12 14
29	20:35:13	14 11	17 50	3 13	11 49	0 29	16 58	19 44	16 47	15 24	18 31	12 14
31	20:43:06	14 04	17 17	6N16	10 47	0N28	17 15	19 45	16 48	15 22	18 30	12 14

Day	☉	☽	☿	♀	♂	♃	♄	♅	♆	♇
● 1	12≈47	11♉39 34	0✶06	28✶52	22♏51	1♊17	24♉07	20≈21	6≈30	14♐43
2	13 42 39	24 56 45	0 28	29 44	23 23	1 18	24 08	20 25	6 33	14 45
3	14 43 31	8♊38 27	0 40	0♈36	23 56	1 20	24 09	20 28	6 35	14 46
4	15 44 20	22 45 58	0R41	1 27	24 29	1 22	24 10	20 32	6 37	14 48
5	16 45 09	7♋18 33	0 31	2 17	25 01	1 24	24 11	20 35	6 39	14 49
6	17 45 56	22 12 47	0 09	3 06	25 34	1 26	24 12	20 38	6 42	14 50
7	18 46 42	7♌22 16	29≈38	3 55	26 06	1 29	24 14	20 42	6 44	14 52
☉ 8	19 47 26	22 33 00	28 56	4 42	26 39	1 32	24 15	20 45	6 46	14 53
9	20 48 10	7♍49 44	28 06	5 29	27 10	1 35	24 17	20 49	6 48	14 54
10	21 48 51	22 47 14	27 08	6 15	27 42	1 38	24 19	20 52	6 50	14 55
11	22 49 32	7♏22 19	26 04	6 59	28 14	1 41	24 21	20 56	6 53	14 56
12	23 50 12	21 29 48	24 57	7 43	28 46	1 45	24 23	20 59	6 55	14 58
13	24 50 50	5♏07 46	23 47	8 25	29 18	1 48	24 25	21 03	6 57	14 59
14	25 51 27	18 17 11	22 37	9 06	29 49	1 52	24 27	21 06	6 59	15 00
● 15	26 52 04	1♐01 10	21 29	9 47	0♐21	1 56	24 29	21 10	7 01	15 01
16	27 52 39	13 24 02	20 24	10 26	0 52	2 01	24 32	21 13	7 04	15 02
17	28 53 12	25 30 46	19 24	11 03	1 23	2 05	24 34	21 17	7 06	15 03
18	29 53 45	7♑26 16	18 29	11 40	1 54	2 10	24 37	21 20	7 08	15 04
19	0✶54 16	19 15 11	17 41	12 15	2 25	2 14	24 40	21 24	7 10	15 05
20	1 54 46	1≈01 33	17 00	12 48	2 56	2 19	24 43	21 27	7 12	15 06
21	2 55 14	12 48 46	16 26	13 20	3 27	2 25	24 46	21 30	7 14	15 06
22	3 55 41	24 39 29	16 00	13 51	3 57	2 30	24 49	21 34	7 16	15 07
● 23	4 56 06	6✶35 05	15 41	14 20	4 28	2 35	24 52	21 37	7 18	15 08
24	5 56 30	18 39 06	15 29	14 47	4 58	2 41	24 55	21 41	7 21	15 09
25	6 56 51	0♈50 43	15 25	15 13	5 28	2 47	24 58	21 44	7 23	15 09
26	7 57 11	13 11 42	15D27	15 37	5 58	2 53	25 02	21 48	7 25	15 10
27	8 57 29	25 43 20	15 36	15 59	6 27	2 59	25 05	21 51	7 27	15 11
28	9 57 45	8♉27 07	15 50	16 19	6 57	3 05	25 09	21 54	7 29	15 11

Day	Sidereal Time	☽ Node	DECLINATIONS									
	H M S		☉	☽	☿	♀	♂	♃	♄	♅	♆	♇
1	20:47:03	14♋01	17S00	10N52	10S19	0N56	17S24	19N45	16N49	15S21	18S29	12S14
3	20:54:56	13 55	16 25	18 39	9 35	1 53	17 41	19 46	16 50	15 18	18 28	12 14
5	21:02:49	13 48	15 49	22 31	9 07	2 48	17 58	19 48	16 51	15 16	18 27	12 14
7	21:10:42	13 42	15 12	20 20	8 57	3 43	18 14	19 49	16 52	15 14	18 26	12 14
9	21:18:35	13 36	14 34	12 28	9 05	4 36	18 30	19 51	16 53	15 12	18 24	12 14
11	21:26:29	13 29	13 54	1 48	9 29	5 28	18 45	19 52	16 55	15 10	18 24	12 14
13	21:34:22	13 23	13 14	8S39	10 06	6 19	19 00	19 54	16 56	15 07	18 23	12 13
15	21:42:15	13 17	12 33	16 51	10 51	7 09	19 14	19 56	16 58	15 05	18 22	12 13
17	21:50:08	13 10	11 52	21 39	11 39	7 56	19 28	19 57	17 00	15 03	18 20	12 13
19	21:58:02	13 04	11 09	22 27	12 26	8 42	19 42	20 01	17 01	15 01	18 19	12 12
21	22:05:54	12 57	10 26	19 17	13 09	9 26	19 55	20 03	17 03	14 59	18 18	12 12
23	22:13:47	12 51	9 42	12 53	13 45	10 08	20 07	20 06	17 05	14 56	18 17	12 12
25	22:21:40	12 45	8 58	4 13	14 15	10 47	20 19	20 08	17 08	14 54	18 16	12 11
27	22:29:33	12 38	8 13	5N18	14 37	11 23	20 31	20 11	17 10	14 52	18 15	12 11

Day	☉	☽	☿	♀	♂	♃	♄	♅	♆	♇
1	10♓57 59	21♉25 02	16≈11	16♈37	7♐26	3♊12	25♉13	21≈58	7≈31	15♐12
2	11 58 11	4♊39 17	16 36	16 53	7 56	3 19	25 17	22 01	7 33	15 12
● 3	12 58 21	18 12 10	17 07	17 07	8 25	3 25	25 21	22 04	7 35	15 13
4	13 58 29	2♋05 30	17 42	17 19	8 53	3 32	25 25	22 08	7 36	15 13
5	14 58 35	16 20 03	18 21	17 29	9 22	3 39	25 29	22 11	7 38	15 13
6	15 58 39	0♌54 40	19 04	17 36	9 51	3 47	25 33	22 14	7 40	15 14
7	16 58 40	15 45 46	19 51	17 41	10 19	3 54	25 37	22 17	7 42	15 15
8	17 58 40	0♍46 59	20 42	17 43	10 47	4 02	25 42	22 21	7 44	15 15
☉ 9	18 58 37	15 49 43	21 35	17R43	11 15	4 09	25 46	22 24	7 46	15 15
10	19 58 33	0♎44 15	22 32	17 41	11 43	4 17	25 51	22 27	7 48	15 16
11	20 58 26	15 21 33	23 31	17 36	12 10	4 25	25 55	22 30	7 49	15 16
12	21 58 18	29 34 39	24 33	17 29	12 38	4 33	26 00	22 33	7 51	15 16
13	22 58 08	13♏19 39	25 38	17 19	13 05	4 42	26 05	22 36	7 53	15 16
14	23 57 56	26 35 49	26 45	17 07	13 32	4 50	26 10	22 39	7 55	15 16
15	24 57 43	9♐25 07	27 54	16 52	13 58	4 59	26 15	22 43	7 56	15 17
☽ 16	25 57 28	21 51 23	29 05	16 35	14 25	5 07	26 20	22 46	7 58	15 17
17	26 57 12	3♑59 30	0♓18	16 15	14 51	5 16	26 25	22 49	8 00	15 17
18	27 56 53	15 55 20	1 33	15 53	15 17	5 25	26 30	22 52	8 01	15 17
19	28 56 33	27 43 59	2 50	15 29	15 43	5 34	26 35	22 55	8 03	15R17
20	29 56 11	9≈30 37	4 09	15 03	16 08	5 43	26 41	22 58	8 05	15 17
21	0♈55 48	21 19 43	5 29	14 34	16 33	5 52	26 46	23 01	8 06	15 16
22	1 55 22	3♓14 15	6 51	14 04	16 58	6 02	26 51	23 03	8 08	15 16
23	2 54 54	15 18 55	8 15	13 32	17 23	6 11	26 57	23 06	8 09	15 16
24	3 54 25	27 33 28	9 40	12 59	17 47	6 21	27 03	23 09	8 11	15 16
● 25	4 53 53	9♈59 29	11 07	12 25	18 11	6 31	27 08	23 12	8 12	15 15
26	5 53 20	22 37 11	12 35	11 49	18 35	6 41	27 14	23 15	8 14	15 15
27	6 52 44	5♉26 22	14 05	11 12	18 59	6 51	27 20	23 18	8 15	15 15
28	7 52 06	18 26 49	15 36	10 35	19 22	7 01	27 26	23 20	8 16	15 15
29	8 51 26	1♊38 31	17 09	9 57	19 45	7 11	27 32	23 23	8 18	15 14
30	9 50 44	15 01 51	18 43	9 20	20 07	7 21	27 38	23 26	8 19	15 14
31	10 50 00	28 37 38	20 18	8 42	20 29	7 32	27 44	23 28	8 20	15 14

Day	Sidereal Time	☽ Node	DECLINATIONS									
	H M S		☉	☽	☿	♀	♂	♃	♄	♅	♆	♇
1	22:37:27	12♋32	7S27	14N13	14S52	11N56	20S42	20N14	17N12	14S50	18S14	12S11
3	22:45:20	12 26	6 41	20 44	15 00	12 26	20 53	20 17	17 14	14 48	18 13	12 10
5	22:53:13	12 19	5 55	22 41	15 00	12 52	21 03	20 20	17 17	14 46	18 12	12 10
7	23:01:06	12 13	5 09	18 42	14 54	13 14	21 14	20 23	17 19	14 44	18 11	12 09
9	23:08:59	12 07	4 22	9 43	14 41	13 32	21 23	20 26	17 22	14 41	18 10	12 09
11	23:16:52	12 00	3 35	1S24	14 22	13 44	21 32	20 30	17 24	14 39	18 10	12 08
13	23:24:45	11 54	2 47	11 41	13 56	13 51	21 41	20 33	17 27	14 37	18 09	12 08
15	23:32:38	11 48	2 00	19 08	13 25	13 53	21 50	20 37	17 30	14 35	18 08	12 07
17	23:40:31	11 41	1 13	22 38	12 48	13 49	21 58	20 40	17 33	14 34	18 07	12 07
19	23:48:24	11 35	0 25	21 55	12 06	13 39	22 06	20 44	17 35	14 32	18 06	12 06
21	23:56:18	11 22	0N22	17 24	11 18	13 22	22 13	20 47	17 38	14 30	18 05	12 06
23	0:04:11	11 22	1 10	9 55	10 25	13 00	22 20	20 51	17 41	14 28	18 05	12 05
25	0:12:04	11 16	1 57	0 38	9 26	12 32	22 27	20 55	17 44	14 26	18 04	12 05
27	0:19:57	11 09	2 44	9N02	8 23	11 59	22 34	20 58	17 47	14 24	18 03	12 04
29	0:27:50	11 03	3 31	17 22	7 15	11 22	22 40	21 02	17 50	14 23	18 02	12 04
31	0:35:43	10 57	4 17	22 22	6 03	10 41	22 46	21 06	17 53	14 21	18 02	12 03

APRIL 2001 — Noon Greenwich Mean Time

Day	☉ ° ' "	☽ ° ' "	☿ ° '	♀ ° '	♂ ° '	♃ ° '	♄ ° '	♅ ° '	♆ ° '	♇ ° '
◐ 1	11♈49 13	12♋26 48	21♓55	8R04	20♐51	7♊42	27♉50	23♒31	8♒22	15R13
2	12 48 24	26 30 01	23 33	7♈28	21 13	7 53	27 56	23 33	8 23	15♐13
3	13 47 32	10♌46 59	25 13	6 52	21 34	8 03	28 03	23 36	8 24	15 12
4	14 46 38	25 15 54	26 54	6 17	21 55	8 14	28 09	23 38	8 25	15 12
5	15 45 42	9♍52 57	28 37	5 43	22 15	8 25	28 15	23 41	8 26	15 11
6	16 44 44	24 32 21	0♈21	5 11	22 35	8 36	28 22	23 43	8 27	15 10
7	17 43 43	9♎06 57	2 06	4 41	22 55	8 47	28 28	23 46	8 29	15 10
○ 8	18 42 40	23 29 19	3 53	4 12	23 14	8 58	28 35	23 48	8 30	15 09
9	19 41 35	7♏32 59	5 42	3 46	23 33	9 10	28 41	23 50	8 31	15 08
10	20 40 29	21 13 31	7 32	3 21	23 52	9 21	28 48	23 53	8 32	15 08
11	21 39 21	4♐28 58	9 23	2 59	24 10	9 32	28 55	23 55	8 33	15 07
12	22 38 10	17 19 51	11 16	2 39	24 27	9 44	29 01	23 57	8 34	15 06
13	23 36 59	29 48 47	13 10	2 22	24 45	9 55	29 08	23 59	8 35	15 05
14	24 35 45	11♑59 52	15 06	2 07	25 01	10 07	29 15	24 01	8 35	15 04
◑ 15	25 34 30	23 58 06	17 04	1 54	25 18	10 19	29 22	24 03	8 36	15 04
16	26 33 13	5♒48 53	19 03	1 44	25 34	10 31	29 29	24 05	8 37	15 03
17	27 31 54	17 37 40	21 03	1 36	25 49	10 42	29 36	24 07	8 38	15 02
18	28 30 33	29 29 34	23 05	1 31	26 04	10 54	29 43	24 09	8 39	15 01
19	29 29 11	11♓29 03	25 08	1 28	26 18	11 06	29 50	24 11	8 39	15 00
20	0♉27 47	23 39 47	27 12	1D27	26 32	11 19	29 57	24 13	8 40	14 59
21	1 26 21	6♈04 20	29 17	1 29	26 45	11 31	0♊04	24 15	8 41	14 58
22	2 24 54	18 44 07	1♉24	1 34	26 58	11 43	0 11	24 17	8 41	14 57
● 23	3 23 25	1♉39 19	3 31	1 40	27 10	11 55	0 19	24 18	8 42	14 56
24	4 21 53	14 49 07	5 39	1 49	27 22	12 08	0 26	24 20	8 42	14 55
25	5 20 20	28 11 56	7 47	2 00	27 33	12 20	0 33	24 22	8 43	14 53
26	6 18 45	11♊45 54	9 56	2 13	27 43	12 33	0 40	24 23	8 43	14 52
27	7 17 09	25 29 14	12 05	2 27	27 53	12 45	0 48	24 25	8 44	14 51
28	8 15 30	9♋20 29	14 13	2 44	28 02	12 58	0 55	24 27	8 44	14 50
29	9 13 49	23 18 38	16 21	3 03	28 11	13 10	1 02	24 28	8 45	14 49
◐ 30	10 12 06	7♌22 54	18 28	3 24	28 19	13 23	1 10	24 29	8 45	14 47

Day	Sidereal Time	☽ Node	DECLINATIONS									
	H M S	° '	☉ ° '	☽ ° '	☿ ° '	♀ ° '	♂ ° '	♃ ° '	♄ ° '	♅ ° '	♆ ° '	♇ ° '
1	0:39:40	10♋54	4N40	23N00	5S25	10N19	22S49	21N08	17N55	14S20	18S01	12S03
3	0:47:33	10 47	5 26	19 58	4 05	9 35	22 55	21 11	17 58	14 18	18 01	12 02
5	0:55:26	10 41	6 12	11 52	2 42	8 49	23 01	21 15	18 01	14 17	18 00	12 02
7	1:03:19	10 34	6 57	1 00	1 14	8 04	23 07	21 19	18 04	14 15	18 00	12 01
9	1:11:12	10 28	7 42	9S50	0N18	7 20	23 12	21 23	18 08	14 14	17 59	12 01
11	1:19:05	10 22	8 26	18 11	1 53	6 37	23 17	21 26	18 11	14 12	17 59	12 00
13	1:26:58	10 15	9 10	22 36	3 32	5 58	23 23	21 30	18 14	14 11	17 58	11 59
15	1:34:51	10 09	9 53	22 34	5 14	5 21	23 28	21 34	18 17	14 10	17 58	11 59
17	1:42:45	10 03	10 36	18 32	6 58	4 49	23 33	21 37	18 21	14 08	17 57	11 58
19	1:50:38	9 56	11 17	11 23	8 44	4 20	23 38	21 41	18 24	14 07	17 57	11 58
21	1:58:31	9 50	11 58	2 13	10 31	3 56	23 43	21 45	18 27	14 06	17 57	11 57
23	2:06:24	9 44	12 39	7N41	12 17	3 36	23 49	21 48	18 30	14 05	17 56	11 57
25	2:14:17	9 37	13 18	16 35	14 02	3 20	23 54	21 52	18 34	14 04	17 56	11 56
27	2:22:10	9 31	13 57	22 15	15 43	3 08	23 59	21 55	18 37	14 03	17 56	11 56
29	2:30:03	9 25	14 34	22 45	17 20	3 01	24 05	21 59	18 40	14 02	17 56	11 55

MAY 2001 — Noon Greenwich Mean Time

Day	☉	☽	☿	♀	♂	♃	♄	♅	♆	♇
1	11ŏ10 20	21♌32 25	20♉33	3♈46	28♐26	13♊36	1♊17	24♒31	8≈45	14R46
2	12 08 33	5♍45 47	22 38	4 10	28 33	13 49	1 25	24 32	8 46	14✓45
3	13 06 44	20 00 41	24 40	4 36	28 39	14 02	1 32	24 33	8 46	14 44
4	14 04 52	4♎13 48	26 40	5 03	28 44	14 14	1 40	24 35	8 46	14 42
5	15 02 59	18 20 58	28 38	5 32	28 49	14 27	1 47	24 36	8 46	14 41
6	16 01 04	2♏17 38	0♊34	6 03	28 53	14 40	1 55	24 37	8 47	14 40
☉ 7	16 59 07	15 59 35	2 27	6 35	28 57	14 53	2 03	24 38	8 47	14 38
8	17 57 09	29 32 37	4 16	7 08	28 59	15 07	2 10	24 39	8 47	14 37
9	18 55 09	12♐27 58	6 03	7 42	29 01	15 20	2 18	24 40	8 47	14 35
10	19 53 08	25 12 30	7 47	8 18	29 02	15 33	2 25	24 41	8 47	14 34
11	20 51 05	7♑38 45	9 27	8 55	29 03	15 46	2 33	24 42	8R47	14 33
12	21 49 01	19 49 35	11 04	9 34	29R03	15 59	2 41	24 43	8 47	14 31
13	22 46 55	1≈48 54	12 37	10 13	29 02	16 13	2 48	24 44	8 47	14 30
14	23 44 49	13 41 18	14 06	10 53	29 00	16 26	2 56	24 45	8 47	14 28
☽ 15	24 42 41	25 31 50	15 32	11 35	28 57	16 39	3 04	24 45	8 47	14 27
16	25 40 31	7♓25 33	16 55	12 17	28 54	16 53	3 12	24 46	8 46	14 25
17	26 38 21	19 27 23	18 13	13 01	28 50	17 06	3 19	24 47	8 46	14 24
18	27 36 09	1♈41 40	19 28	13 45	28 45	17 20	3 27	24 47	8 46	14 22
19	28 33 56	14 12 00	20 39	14 31	28 40	17 33	3 35	24 48	8 46	14 21
20	29 31 43	27 00 49	21 46	15 17	28 33	17 47	3 43	24 48	8 45	14 19
21	0♊29 27	10ŏ09 22	22 49	16 04	28 26	18 00	3 50	24 49	8 45	14 18
22	1 27 11	23 36 35	23 48	16 51	28 18	18 14	3 58	24 49	8 45	14 16
☉ 23	2 24 54	7♊21 14	24 43	17 40	28 10	18 27	4 06	24 49	8 44	14 14
24	3 22 35	21 20 00	25 34	18 29	28 01	18 41	4 14	24 50	8 44	14 13
25	4 20 15	5♋29 08	26 20	19 19	27 50	18 55	4 21	24 50	8 44	14 11
26	5 17 53	19 44 04	27 03	20 10	27 40	19 08	4 29	24 50	8 43	14 10
27	6 15 30	4♌02 45	27 40	21 01	27 29	19 22	4 37	24 50	8 43	14 08
28	7 13 06	18 20 17	28 13	21 53	27 16	19 36	4 45	24 50	8 42	14 06
☽ 29	8 10 40	2♍34 34	28 42	22 45	27 03	19 49	4 53	24 50	8 41	14 05
30	9 08 13	16 43 27	29 06	23 38	26 50	20 03	5 00	24R50	8 41	14 03
31	10 05 44	0♎45 06	29 26	24 32	26 36	20 17	5 08	24 50	8 40	14 02

Day	Sidereal Time H M S	☽ Node	DECLINATIONS ☉	☽	☿	♀	♂	♃	♄	♅	♆	♇
1	2:37:56	9♋18	15N11	17N39	18N50	2N57	24S10	22N02	18N43	14S01	17S55	11S55
3	2:45:49	9 12	15 46	8 25	20 12	2 57	24 16	22 05	18 47	14 00	17 55	11 54
5	2:53:43	9 05	16 21	2S33	21 25	3 00	24 22	22 09	18 50	13 59	17 55	11 54
7	3:01:36	8 59	16 54	12 48	22 28	3 07	24 28	22 12	18 53	13 59	17 55	11 53
9	3:09:29	8 53	17 27	20 09	23 22	3 17	24 35	22 15	18 56	13 58	17 55	11 53
11	3:17:22	8 46	17 58	23 16	24 05	3 29	24 41	22 18	18 59	13 58	17 55	11 52
13	3:25:15	8 40	18 28	21 52	24 38	3 45	24 48	22 21	19 03	13 57	17 55	11 52
15	3:33:08	8 34	18 57	16 39	25 03	4 03	24 54	22 24	19 06	13 57	17 55	11 52
17	3:41:01	8 27	19 24	8 42	25 18	4 23	25 01	22 27	19 09	13 56	17 55	11 51
19	3:48:54	8 21	19 50	0N52	25 26	4 46	25 08	22 30	19 12	13 56	17 55	11 51
21	3:56:47	8 15	20 15	10 45	25 27	5 10	25 16	22 32	19 15	13 56	17 56	11 50
23	4:04:41	8 08	20 39	19 11	25 21	5 36	25 23	22 35	19 18	13 56	17 56	11 50
25	4:12:34	8 02	21 01	23 13	25 09	6 04	25 30	22 38	19 21	13 56	17 56	11 50
27	4:20:27	7 56	21 21	21 35	24 52	6 33	25 37	22 40	19 24	13 56	17 56	11 50
29	4:28:20	7 49	21 41	14 36	24 31	7 03	25 44	22 43	19 27	13 56	17 57	11 49
31	4:36:13	7 43	21 58	4 28	24 06	7 35	25 51	22 45	19 30	13 56	17 57	11 49

Day	☉	☽	☿	♀	♂	♃	♄	♅	♆	♇
1	11Ⅱ03 14	14♎37 47	29Ⅱ41	25♈26	26R21	20Ⅱ31	5Ⅱ16	24R50	8R40	14R00
2	12 00 43	28 19 50	29 51	26 20	26✓06	20 45	5 24	24♒50	8♒39	13✓58
3	12 58 10	11♏49 38	29 57	27 15	25 50	20 58	5 31	24 50	8 38	13 57
4	13 55 36	25 05 47	29R58	28 11	25 34	21 12	5 39	24 49	8 37	13 55
5	14 53 02	8✓07 16	29 54	29 07	25 17	21 26	5 47	24 49	8 37	13 54
☽ 6	15 50 26	20 53 39	29 46	0♋04	25 00	21 40	5 54	24 49	8 36	13 52
7	16 47 50	3♑25 15	29 34	1 01	24 43	21 54	6 02	24 48	8 35	13 50
8	17 45 13	15 43 14	29 18	1 58	24 25	22 07	6 10	24 48	8 34	13 49
9	18 42 35	27 49 35	28 58	2 56	24 06	22 21	6 17	24 47	8 33	13 47
10	19 39 56	9♒47 06	28 35	3 54	23 48	22 35	6 25	24 47	8 32	13 45
11	20 37 17	21 39 19	28 09	4 53	23 29	22 49	6 33	24 46	8 31	13 44
12	21 34 38	3♓30 11	27 40	5 52	23 10	23 03	6 41	24 46	8 30	13 42
13	22 31 57	15 24 15	27 09	6 51	22 52	23 17	6 48	24 45	8 29	13 41
☽ 14	23 29 17	27 26 08	26 37	7 51	22 33	23 30	6 55	24 44	8 28	13 39
15	24 26 36	9♈40 25	26 03	8 51	22 12	23 44	7 03	24 43	8 27	13 38
16	25 23 54	22 11 20	25 29	9 51	21 52	23 58	7 11	24 43	8 26	13 36
17	26 21 13	5♉02 25	24 56	10 52	21 32	24 12	7 18	24 42	8 25	13 34
18	27 18 31	18 16 02	24 21	11 53	21 13	24 26	7 26	24 41	8 24	13 33
19	28 15 49	1Ⅱ53 02	23 50	12 54	20 53	24 40	7 33	24 40	8 23	13 31
20	29 13 06	15 52 23	23 20	13 55	20 34	24 53	7 40	24 39	8 22	13 30
☀ 21	0♋10 23	0♋11 03	22 53	14 57	20 15	25 07	7 48	24 38	8 21	13 28
22	1 07 40	14 44 14	22 27	15 59	19 56	25 21	7 55	24 37	8 20	13 27
23	2 04 56	29 25 50	22 06	17 02	19 38	25 35	8 03	24 36	8 18	13 25
24	3 02 12	14♌09 12	21 47	18 04	19 20	25 49	8 10	24 34	8 17	13 24
25	3 59 27	28 48 01	21 33	19 07	19 02	26 02	8 17	24 33	8 16	13 22
26	4 56 41	13♏16 57	21 23	20 10	18 44	26 16	8 25	24 32	8 15	13 21
27	5 53 55	27 32 07	21 17	21 13	18 28	26 30	8 32	24 31	8 13	13 19
☽ 28	6 51 08	11♎31 13	21 16	22 17	18 11	26 44	8 39	24 29	8 12	13 18
29	7 48 21	25 13 14	21D20	23 21	17 55	26 57	8 46	24 28	8 11	13 16
30	8 45 33	8♏38 17	21 28	24 24	17 40	27 11	8 53	24 27	8 09	13 15

Day	Sidereal Time	Node	DECLINATIONS									
			☉	☽	☿	♀	♂	♃	♄	♅	♆	♇
	H M S	° '	° '	° '	° '	° '	° '	° '	° '	° '	° '	° '
1	4:40:10	7♋40	22N06	0S59	23N52	7N51	25S55	22N46	19N31	13S56	17S57	11S49
3	4:48:03	7 33	22 11	11 19	23 22	8 24	26 02	22 48	19 34	13 56	17 57	11 49
5	4:55:56	7 27	22 35	19 12	22 50	8 58	26 08	22 50	19 36	13 56	17 58	11 49
7	5:03:49	7 21	22 47	23 08	22 16	9 32	26 14	22 52	19 39	13 57	17 59	11 48
9	5:11:42	7 14	22 58	22 29	21 42	10 07	26 20	22 54	19 42	13 57	17 59	11 48
11	5:19:35	7 08	23 06	17 50	21 07	10 42	26 25	22 55	19 44	13 57	17 59	11 48
13	5:27:28	7 02	23 14	10 17	20 34	11 18	26 30	22 57	19 47	13 58	18 00	11 48
15	5:35:21	6 55	23 19	1 01	20 03	11 53	26 34	22 58	19 50	13 58	18 00	11 48
17	5:43:14	6 49	23 23	8N50	19 35	12 29	26 38	23 00	19 52	13 59	18 01	11 48
19	5:51:08	6 43	23 26	17 36	19 12	13 04	26 41	23 01	19 55	14 00	18 01	11 48
21	5:59:01	6 36	23 26	22 52	18 54	13 40	26 44	23 02	19 57	14 01	18 02	11 48
23	6:06:54	6 30	23 25	22 18	18 41	14 15	26 46	23 04	19 59	14 01	18 03	11 48
25	6:14:47	6 23	23 23	15 49	18 36	14 49	26 48	23 05	20 01	14 02	18 03	11 48
27	6:22:40	6 17	23 18	5 46	18 37	15 22	26 50	23 06	20 04	14 03	18 04	11 49
29	6:30:33	6 11	23 13	5S06	18 44	15 55	26 50	23 06	20 06	14 04	18 05	11 49

JULY 2001 — Noon Greenwich Mean Time

Day	☉	☽	☿	♀	♂	♃	♄	♅	♆	♇
1	9♋42 45	21♏47 05	21♋41	25♋29	17R25	27♊25	9♊00	24R25	8R08	13R13
2	10 39 57	4♐40 49	22 00	26 33	17✗11	27 38	9 07	24 24	8 07	13 12
3	11 37 08	17 20 47	22 23	27 37	16 58	27 52	9 14	24 22	8 05	13 11
4	12 34 20	29 48 23	22 51	28 42	16 45	28 06	9 21	24 21	8 04	13 09
5	13 31 31	12♑05 01	23 24	29 47	16 33	28 19	9 28	24 19	8 02	13 08
☽ 6	14 28 42	24 12 17	24 02	0♌52	16 22	28 33	9 35	24 17	8 01	13 07
7	15 25 54	6≈11 55	24 45	1 58	16 11	28 46	9 42	24 16	7 59	13 05
8	16 23 05	18 05 59	25 32	3 03	16 01	29 00	9 49	24 14	7 58	13 04
9	17 20 17	29 57 00	26 24	4 09	15 52	29 13	9 55	24 12	7 56	13 03
10	18 17 29	11♓47 53	27 21	5 14	15 44	29 27	10 02	24 10	7 55	13 02
11	19 14 41	23 42 03	28 22	6 20	15 37	29 40	10 09	24 09	7 53	13 00
12	20 11 54	5♈43 21	29 29	7 27	15 30	29 53	10 15	24 07	7 52	12 59
☽ 13	21 09 07	17 53 41	0♋39	8 33	15 24	0♋07	10 22	24 05	7 50	12 58
14	22 06 21	0♉24 10	1 54	9 39	15 19	0 20	10 28	24 03	7 49	12 57
15	23 03 36	13 12 05	3 14	10 46	15 15	0 33	10 35	24 01	7 47	12 56
16	24 00 51	26 23 15	4 37	11 53	15 12	0 46	10 41	23 59	7 46	12 55
17	24 58 07	10♊00 01	6 05	13 00	15 09	1 00	10 48	23 57	7 44	12 53
18	25 55 23	24 03 01	7 37	14 07	15 07	1 13	10 54	23 55	7 42	12 52
19	26 52 40	8♋30 34	9 13	15 14	15 07	1 26	11 01	23 53	7 41	12 51
☉ 20	27 49 58	23 18 18	10 53	16 21	15D07	1 39	11 06	23 51	7 39	12 50
21	28 47 16	8♌19 19	12 36	17 29	15 07	1 52	11 12	23 49	7 38	12 49
22	29 44 35	23 24 57	14 23	18 36	15 09	2 05	11 18	23 47	7 36	12 48
23	0♌41 53	8♍25 56	16 13	19 44	15 12	2 18	11 23	23 45	7 34	12 47
24	1 39 13	23 13 52	18 05	20 52	15 15	2 31	11 30	23 43	7 33	12 46
25	2 36 32	7♎42 27	20 01	22 00	15 20	2 44	11 36	23 41	7 31	12 46
26	3 33 52	21 47 55	21 59	23 08	15 25	2 56	11 42	23 38	7 30	12 45
☉ 27	4 31 13	5♏29 07	23 59	24 16	15 30	3 09	11 48	23 36	7 28	12 43
28	5 28 34	18 47 00	26 01	25 25	15 37	3 22	11 53	23 34	7 26	12 43
29	6 25 55	1♐43 53	28 04	26 33	15 45	3 34	11 59	23 32	7 25	12 42
30	7 23 17	14 22 50	0♌09	27 42	15 53	3 47	12 05	23 29	7 23	12 41
31	8 20 39	26 47 07	2 14	28 50	16 02	3 59	12 10	23 27	7 21	12 41

Day	Sidereal Time	☽ Node	DECLINATIONS								
			☉	☽	☿	♀	♂	♃	♄	♅	♆	♇
	H M S	° ′										
1	6:38:26	6♋04	23N05	14S37	18N56	16N27	26S51	23N07	20N08	14S05	18S06	11S49
3	6:46:19	5 58	22 56	21 07	19 14	16 59	26 51	23 08	20 10	14 06	18 06	11 49
5	6:54:12	5 52	22 45	23 25	19 35	17 29	26 51	23 08	20 12	14 07	18 07	11 49
7	7:02:06	5 45	22 33	21 16	20 00	17 58	26 51	23 09	20 14	14 08	18 08	11 49
9	7:09:59	5 39	22 19	15 28	20 27	18 25	26 51	23 09	20 16	14 10	18 09	11 50
11	7:17:52	5 33	22 03	7 13	20 55	18 52	26 51	23 10	20 18	14 11	18 10	11 50
13	7:25:45	5 26	21 47	2N16	21 21	19 17	26 51	23 10	20 20	14 13	18 11	11 51
15	7:33:38	5 20	21 28	11 47	21 46	19 40	26 51	23 10	20 22	14 14	18 11	11 51
17	7:41:31	5 14	21 08	19 38	22 07	20 02	26 50	23 11	20 24	14 15	18 12	11 51
19	7:49:24	5 07	20 47	23 42	22 24	20 22	26 50	23 11	20 26	14 16	18 13	11 52
21	7:57:17	5 01	20 24	23 32	22 36	20 41	26 50	23 11	20 27	14 18	18 13	11 52
23	8:05:10	4 55	20 00	18 42	22 42	20 57	26 50	23 09	20 28	14 19	18 14	11 52
25	8:13:04	4 48	19 35	1 45	22 42	21 12	26 50	23 09	20 29	14 20	18 15	11 53
27	8:20:57	4 42	19 08	9S03	22 08	21 24	26 50	23 09	20 30	14 22	18 16	11 54
29	8:28:50	4 35	18 40	17 37	21 38	21 35	26 51	23 08	20 32	14 23	18 17	11 54
31	8:36:43	4 29	18 11	22 33	20 59	21 43	26 52	23 08	20 33	14 25	18 18	11 55

AUGUST 2001 — Noon Greenwich Mean Time

Day	☉	☽	☿	♀	♂	♃	♄	♅	♆	♇
	° ′ ″	° ′ ″	° ′	° ′	° ′	° ′	° ′	° ′	° ′	° ′
1	9♌18 02	8♑59 54	4♌19	29♊59	16♐12	4♋12	12♊16	23R25	7R20	12R40
2	10 15 26	21 04 00	6 25	1♋08	16 22	4 24	12 21	23♒23	7♒18	12♐39
3	11 12 51	3♒01 50	8 31	2 17	16 34	4 37	12 26	23 20	7 17	12 39
○ 4	12 10 16	14 55 31	10 36	3 26	16 46	4 49	12 31	23 18	7 15	12 38
5	13 07 43	26 46 54	12 40	4 35	16 58	5 01	12 36	23 16	7 13	12 38
6	14 05 10	8♓37 51	14 44	5 45	17 12	5 13	12 41	23 13	7 12	12 37
7	15 02 39	20 30 22	16 47	6 54	17 26	5 25	12 46	23 11	7 10	12 36
8	16 00 09	2♈26 43	18 49	8 04	17 41	5 37	12 51	23 08	7 09	12 36
9	16 57 39	14 29 39	20 49	9 13	17 56	5 49	12 56	23 06	7 07	12 35
10	17 55 12	26 42 23	22 49	10 23	18 12	6 01	13 01	23 04	7 05	12 35
11	18 52 45	9♉08 36	24 47	11 33	18 29	6 13	13 05	23 01	7 04	12 35
◑ 12	19 50 21	21 52 16	26 44	12 43	18 46	6 25	13 10	22 59	7 02	12 34
13	20 47 57	4♊57 17	28 39	13 53	19 04	6 36	13 15	22 57	7 01	12 34
14	21 45 35	18 27 04	0♍33	15 03	19 22	6 48	13 19	22 54	6 59	12 34
15	22 43 15	2♋23 47	2 25	16 13	19 42	6 59	13 23	22 52	6 57	12 33
16	23 40 56	16 47 35	4 16	17 24	20 01	7 11	13 27	22 49	6 56	12 33
17	24 38 39	1♌35 48	6 06	18 34	20 22	7 22	13 32	22 47	6 54	12 33
18	25 36 23	16 42 28	7 54	19 45	20 42	7 34	13 36	22 45	6 53	12 33
● 19	26 34 08	1♍58 43	9 40	20 55	21 04	7 45	13 40	22 42	6 51	12 33
20	27 31 55	17 13 49	11 26	22 06	21 26	7 56	13 44	22 40	6 50	12 32
21	28 29 43	2♎17 01	13 09	23 17	21 48	8 07	13 47	22 37	6 48	12 32
22	29 27 32	16 59 30	14 52	24 28	22 11	8 18	13 51	22 35	6 47	12 32
23	0♍25 22	1♏15 30	16 33	25 38	22 35	8 29	13 55	22 33	6 45	12 32
24	1 23 13	15 02 44	18 13	26 50	22 59	8 39	13 58	22 30	6 44	12D32
◐ 25	2 21 06	28 21 52	19 51	28 01	23 24	8 50	14 02	22 28	6 42	12 32
26	3 19 00	11♐15 48	21 28	29 12	23 49	9 01	14 05	22 26	6 41	12 32
27	4 16 55	23 48 37	23 04	0♌23	24 14	9 11	14 08	22 23	6 40	12 33
28	5 14 52	6♑04 54	24 38	1 34	24 40	9 21	14 11	22 21	6 38	12 33
29	6 12 50	18 09 12	26 11	2 46	25 06	9 32	14 14	22 19	6 37	12 33
30	7 10 49	0♒05 38	27 43	3 57	25 33	9 42	14 17	22 16	6 36	12 33
31	8 08 49	11 57 41	29 13	5 09	26 00	9 52	14 20	22 14	6 34	12 33

Day	Sidereal Time	☽ Node	DECLINATIONS ☉	☽	☿	♀	♂	♃	♄	♅	♆	♇
	H M S	° ′	° ′	° ′	° ′	° ′	° ′	° ′	° ′	° ′	° ′	° ′
1	8:40:39	4♋26	17N56	23S24	20N35	21N46	26S53	23N07	20N34	14S26	18S18	11S55
3	8:48:33	4 20	17 25	21 46	19 41	21 51	26 53	23 07	20 35	14 27	18 19	11 56
5	8:56:26	4 13	16 53	16 21	18 39	21 54	26 54	23 06	20 36	14 29	18 20	11 56
7	9:04:19	4 07	16 19	8 20	17 29	21 54	26 55	23 05	20 37	14 30	18 21	11 57
9	9:12:12	4 00	15 45	1N01	16 13	21 52	26 56	23 04	20 38	14 32	18 22	11 58
11	9:20:05	3 54	15 10	10 28	14 53	21 48	26 57	23 03	20 39	14 34	18 22	11 58
13	9:27:58	3 48	14 34	18 33	13 29	21 42	26 58	23 02	20 40	14 35	18 23	11 59
15	9:35:51	3 41	13 56	23 09	12 03	21 33	26 59	23 01	20 41	14 37	18 24	12 00
17	9:43:44	3 35	13 18	22 01	10 34	21 21	27 00	23 00	20 42	14 38	18 25	12 01
19	9:51:37	3 29	12 40	14 46	9 04	21 07	27 01	22 59	20 42	14 40	18 26	12 01
21	9:59:31	3 22	12 00	3 46	7 34	20 51	27 01	22 58	20 43	14 41	18 26	12 02
23	10:07:24	3 16	11 19	7S37	6 04	20 33	27 01	22 57	20 44	14 43	18 27	12 03
25	10:15:17	3 10	10 38	16 50	4 34	20 12	27 02	22 55	20 44	14 45	18 28	12 04
27	10:23:10	3 03	9 56	22 20	3 04	19 49	27 01	22 54	20 45	14 46	18 29	12 05
29	10:31:03	2 57	9 14	23 23	1 36	19 24	27 01	22 53	20 45	14 48	18 29	12 06
31	10:38:56	2 51	8 31	20 10	0 09	18 56	27 00	22 52	20 46	14 49	18 30	12 07

Day	☉	☽	☿	♀	♂	♃	♄	♅	♆	♇
1	9♍06 51	23♒48 13	0♎42	6♌21	26♐28	10♋02	14♊23	22R12	6R33	12♐34
2 ⊗	10 04 55	5♓29 25	2 10	7 32	26 56	10 21	14 26	22♒09	6♒32	12 34
3	11 03 00	17 33 01	3 36	8 44	27 25	10 40	14 28	22 07	6 30	12 34
4	12 01 07	29 30 26	5 01	9 56	27 53	10 59	14 31	22 05	6 29	12 35
5	12 59 16	11♈33 04	6 25	11 08	28 23	11 17	14 33	22 03	6 28	12 35
6	13 57 27	23 37 23	7 47	12 20	28 52	11 35	14 35	22 01	6 27	12 36
7	14 55 39	6♉00 40	9 07	13 32	29 22	11 52	14 37	21 59	6 25	12 36
8	15 53 53	18 30 09	10 27	14 45	29 53	12 09	14 39	21 57	6 24	12 36
9	16 52 10	1♊13 56	11 44	15 57	0♑23	12 25	14 41	21 54	6 23	12 37
10 ◐	17 50 29	14 15 26	13 00	17 09	0 54	12 41	14 43	21 52	6 22	12 37
11	18 48 49	27 38 03	14 15	18 22	1 26	12 56	14 45	21 50	6 21	12 38
12	19 47 12	11♋24 36	15 28	19 34	1 57	13 11	14 47	21 48	6 20	12 39
13	20 45 37	25 36 31	16 39	20 47	2 29	13 25	14 48	21 46	6 19	12 39
14	21 44 05	10♌12 57	17 48	22 00	3 01	13 39	14 50	21 44	6 18	12 40
15	22 42 34	25 09 58	18 55	23 12	3 34	13 52	14 51	21 42	6 17	12 41
16	23 41 05	10♍20 13	20 00	24 25	4 07	14 05	14 52	21 40	6 16	12 42
17 ○	24 39 38	25 33 55	21 02	25 38	4 40	14 17	14 53	21 38	6 15	12 42
18	25 38 13	10♎40 01	22 03	26 51	5 14	14 29	14 54	21 37	6 14	12 43
19	26 36 50	25 28 25	23 00	28 04	5 48	14 40	14 55	21 35	6 13	12 44
20	27 35 28	9♏51 39	23 55	29 17	6 22	14 51	14 56	21 33	6 12	12 45
21	28 34 09	23 45 46	24 47	0♍30	6 56	15 01	14 56	21 31	6 11	12 46
22	29 32 51	7♐10 14	25 36	1 43	7 31	15 11	14 57	21 29	6 10	12 47
23	0♎31 34	20 07 15	26 22	2 56	8 06	15 20	14 57	21 28	6 10	12 48
24 ◑	1 30 20	2♑40 52	27 03	4 10	8 41	15 28	14 58	21 26	6 09	12 49
25	2 29 07	14 56 03	27 40	5 23	9 16	15 36	14 58	21 25	6 08	12 50
26	3 27 56	26 58 04	28 14	6 36	9 52	15 43	14 58	21 23	6 07	12 51
27	4 26 47	8♒51 56	28 42	7 50	10 28	15 50	14 58	21 21	6 07	12 52
28	5 25 39	20 42 10	29 06	9 03	11 04	15 56	14 58	21 20	6 06	12 53
29	6 24 33	2♓32 33	29 24	10 17	11 40	16 01	14 58	21 18	6 05	12 54
30	7 23 29	14 26 02	29 35	11 30	12 17	13 57	14 57	21 17	6 05	12 56

Day	Sidereal Time (H M S)	☽ Node	DECLINATIONS									
			☉	☽	☿	♀	♂	♃	♄	♅	♆	♇
1	10:42:53	2♋47	8N09	17S12	0S34	18N42	27S00	22N51	20N46	14S50	18S30	12S07
3	10:50:46	2 41	7 25	9 22	1 58	18 11	26 58	22 50	20 46	14 51	18 31	12 08
5	10:58:39	2 35	6 41	0 01	3 20	17 38	26 56	22 48	20 47	14 53	18 32	12 09
7	11:06:32	2 28	5 56	9N31	4 40	17 04	26 54	22 47	20 47	14 54	18 32	12 10
9	11:14:25	2 22	5 11	17 47	5 57	16 27	26 51	22 45	20 47	14 55	18 33	12 11
11	11:22:18	2 16	4 26	22 56	7 11	15 48	26 48	22 44	20 47	14 57	18 34	12 12
13	11:30:11	2 09	3 40	22 55	8 22	15 08	26 44	22 43	20 47	14 58	18 34	12 13
15	11:38:04	2 03	2 54	16 52	9 29	14 26	26 40	22 41	20 47	14 59	18 35	12 14
17	11:45:58	1 57	2 07	6 19	10 32	13 42	26 35	22 40	20 47	15 00	18 35	12 15
19	11:53:51	1 50	1 21	5S33	11 30	12 57	26 29	22 39	20 47	15 01	18 36	12 16
21	12:01:44	1 44	0 34	15 42	12 23	12 10	26 23	22 37	20 47	15 03	18 36	12 17
23	12:09:37	1 37	0S13	22 03	13 09	11 21	26 16	22 36	20 47	15 04	18 36	12 18
25	12:17:30	1 31	0 59	23 44	13 48	10 32	26 08	22 35	20 47	15 05	18 37	12 19
27	12:25:23	1 25	1 46	20 58	14 18	9 41	25 59	22 34	20 47	15 06	18 37	12 20
29	12:33:16	1 18	2 33	14 39	14 39	8 49	25 50	22 33	20 46	15 07	18 38	12 21

OCTOBER 2001 — Noon Greenwich Mean Time

Day	☉	☽	☿	♀	♂	♃	♄	♅	♆	♇
	° ′ ″	° ′ ″	° ′	° ′	° ′	° ′	° ′	° ′	° ′	° ′
1	8♎22 27	26♓24 48	29♎41	12♍44	12♑53	14♋03	14R57	21R16	6R04	12♐57
2	9 21 27	8♈30 18	29R39	13 58	13 30	14 09	14♊56	21♒14	6♒04	12 58
3	10 20 29	20 43 31	29 31	15 12	14 08	14 14	14 56	21 13	6 03	12 59
4	11 19 33	3♉05 10	29 15	16 25	14 45	14 20	14 55	21 12	6 03	13 01
5	12 18 39	15 35 59	28 51	17 39	15 22	14 25	14 54	21 10	6 02	13 02
6	13 17 48	28 17 03	28 19	18 53	16 00	14 30	14 53	21 09	6 02	13 03
7	14 16 58	11♊09 50	27 39	20 07	16 38	14 35	14 52	21 08	6 02	13 05
8	15 16 11	24 16 22	26 52	21 21	17 16	14 40	14 51	21 07	6 01	13 06
9	16 15 26	7♋38 56	25 58	22 35	17 55	14 45	14 50	21 06	6 01	13 08
10	17 14 44	21 19 44	24 57	23 50	18 33	14 49	14 48	21 05	6 01	13 09
11	18 14 04	5♌20 13	23 51	25 04	19 12	14 54	14 47	21 04	6 01	13 11
12	19 13 26	19 40 26	22 40	26 18	19 50	14 58	14 45	21 03	6 00	13 12
13	20 12 51	4♍18 11	21 28	27 32	20 29	15 02	14 43	21 02	6 00	13 14
14	21 12 18	19 08 36	20 16	28 47	21 09	15 06	14 42	21 01	6 00	13 15
15	22 11 47	4♎04 21	19 06	0♎01	21 48	15 09	14 40	21 00	6 00	13 17
16	23 11 18	18 56 31	17 59	1 15	22 27	15 13	14 38	21 00	6 00	13 19
17	24 10 51	3♏36 05	16 58	2 30	23 07	15 16	14 35	20 59	6 00	13 20
18	25 10 26	17 55 29	16 05	3 44	23 47	15 19	14 33	20 58	6D00	13 22
19	26 10 03	1♐49 45	15 22	4 59	24 27	15 22	14 31	20 58	6 00	13 24
20	27 09 42	15 16 51	14 48	6 13	25 07	15 24	14 28	20 57	6 00	13 25
21	28 09 23	28 17 35	14 25	7 28	25 47	15 27	14 26	20 57	6 00	13 27
22	29 09 06	10♑54 47	14 14	8 42	26 27	15 29	14 23	20 56	6 00	13 29
23	0♏08 50	23 12 46	14 13	9 57	27 08	15 31	14 20	20 56	6 00	13 31
24	1 08 36	5♒16 34	14D24	11 12	27 48	15 33	14 18	20 56	6 00	13 32
25	2 08 24	17 11 25	14 46	12 26	28 29	15 35	14 15	20 55	6 01	13 34
26	3 08 13	29 02 25	15 17	13 41	29 10	15 36	14 12	20 55	6 01	13 36
27	4 08 04	10♓54 10	15 57	14 56	29 51	15 38	14 09	20 55	6 01	13 38
28	5 07 56	22 50 36	16 45	16 11	0♒32	15 39	14 05	20 55	6 02	13 40
29	6 07 51	4♈54 50	17 41	17 26	1 13	15 40	14 02	20 55	6 02	13 42
30	7 07 47	17 09 02	18 43	18 40	1 54	15 41	13 59	20 55	6 02	13 44
31	8 07 45	29 34 33	19 51	19 55	2 36	15 41	13 55	20D55	6 03	13 46

Day	Sidereal Time	☽ Node	DECLINATIONS ☉	☽	☿	♀	♂	♃	♄	♅	♆	♇
	H M S	° ′	° ′	° ′	° ′	° ′	° ′	° ′	° ′	° ′	° ′	° ′
1	12:41:09	1♋12	3S19	6S00	14S47	7N56	25S40	22N32	20N46	15S07	18S38	12S22
3	12:49:02	1 06	4 06	3N44	14 41	7 02	25 30	22 30	20 46	15 08	18 38	12 23
5	12:56:56	0 59	4 52	13 07	14 19	6 07	25 18	22 30	20 45	15 09	18 38	12 25
7	13:04:49	0 53	5 38	20 29	13 40	5 11	25 06	22 29	20 45	15 10	18 39	12 26
9	13:12:42	0 47	6 24	23 53	12 43	4 15	24 53	22 28	20 44	15 10	18 39	12 27
11	13:20:35	0 40	7 09	21 46	11 29	3 18	24 39	22 27	20 44	15 11	18 39	12 28
13	13:28:28	0 34	7 54	14 10	10 03	2 21	24 25	22 26	20 43	15 11	18 39	12 29
15	13:36:21	0 28	8 39	3 00	8 32	1 23	24 10	22 26	20 43	15 12	18 39	12 30
17	13:44:14	0 21	9 23	8S47	7 06	0 25	23 53	22 25	20 42	15 12	18 39	12 31
19	13:52:07	0 15	10 06	18 15	5 52	0S34	23 36	22 24	20 41	15 13	18 39	12 32
21	14:00:00	0 09	10 49	23 22	4 58	1 32	23 19	22 24	20 41	15 13	18 39	12 33
23	14:07:54	0 02	11 31	23 30	4 26	2 31	23 00	22 24	20 40	15 13	18 39	12 34
25	14:15:47	29♊56	12 13	19 18	4 18	3 29	22 41	22 24	20 39	15 13	18 39	12 35
27	14:23:40	29 49	12 54	11 58	4 31	4 27	22 21	22 23	20 38	15 13	18 39	12 36
29	14:31:33	29 43	13 34	2 42	5 01	5 25	22 00	22 23	20 37	15 13	18 39	12 37
31	14:39:26	29 37	14 13	7N14	5 46	6 23	21 38	22 23	20 36	15 13	18 39	12 38

Day	☉	☽	☿	♀	♂	♃	♄	♅	♆	♇
☽ 1	9♏07 45	12♉11 56	21♎04	21♎10	3≈17	15♋41	13♊52	20≈55	6≈03	13♐48
2	10 07 47	25 01 11	22 21	22 25	3 59	15 41	13♊48	20 55	6 04	13 50
3	11 07 50	8♊02 00	23 41	23 40	4 40	15♋41	13 45	20 55	6 04	13 52
4	12 07 56	21 14 06	25 05	24 55	5 22	15 41	13 41	20 55	6 05	13 54
5	13 08 04	4♋37 24	26 31	26 10	6 04	15 41	13 37	20 55	6 06	13 56
6	14 08 14	18 12 04	28 00	27 25	6 46	15 40	13 33	20 56	6 06	13 58
7	15 08 26	1♌58 24	29 30	28 40	7 28	15 39	13 29	20 56	6 07	14 00
☽ 8	16 08 40	15 56 32	1♏02	29 55	8 10	15 38	13 25	20 56	6 08	14 02
9	17 08 56	0♍06 00	2 34	1♏10	8 52	15 37	13 21	20 57	6 08	14 04
10	18 09 14	14 25 16	4 08	2 26	9 34	15 35	13 17	20 57	6 09	14 06
11	19 09 34	28 51 22	5 42	3 41	10 17	15 34	13 13	20 58	6 10	14 08
12	20 09 56	13♎19 51	7 17	4 56	10 59	15 32	13 08	20 59	6 11	14 10
13	21 10 19	27 45 10	8 52	6 11	11 42	15 30	13 04	20 59	6 12	14 13
14	22 10 45	12♏01 17	10 28	7 26	12 24	15 27	13 00	21 00	6 12	14 15
☽ 15	23 11 12	26 02 41	12 04	8 42	13 07	15 25	12 55	21 01	6 13	14 17
16	24 11 41	9♐45 02	13 40	9 57	13 50	15 22	12 51	21 02	6 14	14 19
17	25 12 12	23 05 54	15 15	11 12	14 32	15 19	12 46	21 02	6 15	14 21
18	26 12 44	6♑04 45	16 51	12 27	15 15	15 16	12 42	21 03	6 16	14 24
19	27 13 17	18 42 54	18 27	13 43	15 58	15 13	12 37	21 04	6 17	14 26
20	28 13 52	1≈03 10	20 03	14 58	16 41	15 10	12 32	21 05	6 19	14 28
21	29 14 27	13 09 27	21 38	16 13	17 24	15 06	12 28	21 06	6 20	14 30
☽ 22	0♐15 04	25 06 17	23 14	17 29	18 07	15 02	12 23	21 07	6 21	14 32
23	1 15 42	6♓58 35	24 49	18 44	18 50	14 58	12 18	21 09	6 22	14 35
24	2 16 22	18 51 16	26 25	19 59	19 34	14 54	12 13	21 10	6 23	14 37
25	3 17 02	0♈48 58	28 00	21 15	20 17	14 50	12 08	21 11	6 24	14 39
26	4 17 43	12 55 51	29 35	22 30	21 00	14 45	12 04	21 12	6 26	14 42
27	5 18 26	25 15 21	1♐09	23 45	21 43	14 40	11 59	21 14	6 27	14 44
28	6 19 09	7♉49 57	2 44	25 01	22 27	14 36	11 54	21 15	6 28	14 46
29	7 19 54	20 41 03	4 19	26 16	23 10	14 31	11 49	21 17	6 30	14 48
☽ 30	8 20 40	3♊48 56	5 53	27 32	23 54	14 25	11 44	21 18	6 31	14 51

Day	Sidereal Time	☽ Node					DECLINATIONS				
	H M S		☉	☽	☿	♀	♂	♃	♄	♅	♆	♇
1	14:43:23	29♊34	14S32	12N00	6S12	6S51	21S27	22N24	20N36	15S13	18S39	12S39
3	14:51:16	29 27	15 10	19 55	7 12	7 48	21 04	22 24	20 35	15 13	18 38	12 40
5	14:59:09	29 21	15 47	23 58	8 18	8 44	20 41	22 24	20 34	15 13	18 38	12 40
7	15:07:02	29 14	16 23	22 33	9 28	9 40	20 17	22 24	20 33	15 13	18 38	12 41
9	15:14:55	29 08	16 57	15 43	10 41	10 34	19 52	22 25	20 32	15 12	18 37	12 42
11	15:22:48	29 02	17 31	5 12	11 54	11 28	19 26	22 25	20 31	15 12	18 37	12 43
13	15:30:41	28 55	18 03	6S29	13 07	12 20	19 00	22 26	20 30	15 11	18 37	12 44
15	15:38:34	28 49	18 34	16 38	14 18	13 12	18 33	22 27	20 29	15 11	18 36	12 45
17	15:46:27	28 43	19 04	22 57	15 28	14 02	18 05	22 28	20 28	15 10	18 36	12 46
19	15:54:21	28 36	19 32	24 01	16 35	14 50	17 37	22 29	20 26	15 10	18 35	12 47
21	16:02:14	28 30	19 59	20 28	17 39	15 37	17 08	22 30	20 25	15 09	18 35	12 48
23	16:10:07	28 24	20 25	13 30	18 41	16 23	16 40	22 31	20 24	15 08	18 34	12 49
25	16:18:00	28 17	20 49	4 28	19 38	17 07	16 09	22 32	20 23	15 07	18 34	12 49
27	16:25:53	28 11	21 11	5N27	20 32	17 49	15 38	22 33	20 21	15 06	18 33	12 50
29	16:33:46	28 05	21 32	14 54	21 22	18 29	15 07	22 35	20 21	15 05	18 32	12 51

56

DECEMBER 2001 — Noon Greenwich Mean Time

Day	☉	☽	☿	♀	♂	♃	♄	♅	♆	♇
1	9♐21 28	17♉12 46	7♐28	28♏47	24♒37	14R20	11R39	21♒20	6♒32	14♐53
2	10 22 16	0♊50 50	9 02	0♐02	25 20	14S14	11♈34	21 21	6 34	14 55
3	11 23 06	14 40 49	10 36	1 18	26 04	14 09	11 29	21 23	6 35	14 58
4	12 23 57	28 40 02	12 11	2 33	26 48	14 03	11 24	21 25	6 37	15 00
5	13 24 50	12♋45 49	13 45	3 49	27 31	13 57	11 19	21 26	6 38	15 02
6	14 25 43	26 55 37	15 19	5 04	28 15	13 51	11 14	21 28	6 40	15 05
7	15 26 38	11♌07 07	16 53	6 20	28 58	13 44	11 10	21 30	6 42	15 07
8	16 27 34	25 18 06	18 27	7 35	29 42	13 38	11 05	21 32	6 43	15 09
9	17 28 32	9♍26 26	20 02	8 51	0♓25	13 31	11 00	21 34	6 45	15 11
10	18 29 30	23 29 49	21 36	10 06	1 09	13 25	10 55	21 36	6 46	15 14
11	19 30 30	7♎25 53	23 10	11 22	1 53	13 18	10 50	21 38	6 48	15 16
12	20 31 31	21 12 10	24 45	12 37	2 37	13 11	10 45	21 40	6 50	15 18
13	21 32 33	4♏46 18	26 19	13 53	3 21	13 04	10 40	21 42	6 51	15 21
14	22 33 36	18 06 18	27 54	15 08	4 04	12 57	10 36	21 44	6 53	15 23
15	23 34 39	1♐10 44	29 29	16 24	4 48	12 50	10 31	21 46	6 55	15 25
16	24 35 44	13 59 02	1♑03	17 39	5 32	12 42	10 26	21 48	6 57	15 28
17	25 36 49	26 31 35	2 38	18 55	6 16	12 35	10 21	21 51	6 59	15 30
18	26 37 54	8♑49 49	4 13	20 10	7 00	12 27	10 17	21 53	7 00	15 32
19	27 39 00	20 56 04	5 49	21 26	7 44	12 20	10 12	21 55	7 02	15 34
20	28 40 06	2♒53 35	7 24	22 41	8 28	12 12	10 08	21 58	7 04	15 37
21	29 41 12	14 46 15	8 59	23 57	9 12	12 04	10 03	22 00	7 06	15 39
22	0♑42 18	26 36 20	10 35	25 12	9 56	11 56	9 59	22 02	7 08	15 41
23	1 43 25	8♓34 55	12 10	26 28	10 39	11 48	9 54	22 05	7 10	15 43
24	2 44 32	20 40 51	13 45	27 43	11 23	11 41	9 50	22 07	7 12	15 46
25	3 45 39	2♈59 16	15 21	28 59	12 07	11 33	9 46	22 10	7 14	15 48
26	4 46 46	15 35 36	16 56	0♑14	12 51	11 25	9 41	22 12	7 16	15 50
27	5 47 53	28 32 24	18 31	1 30	13 35	11 16	9 37	22 15	7 18	15 52
28	6 49 01	11♉51 23	20 06	2 45	14 19	11 08	9 33	22 17	7 20	15 54
29	7 50 08	25 32 32	21 41	4 01	15 03	11 00	9 29	22 21	7 22	15 57
30	8 51 16	9♊34 14	23 15	5 16	15 47	10 52	9 25	22 23	7 24	15 59
31	9 52 23	23 52 34	24 48	6 32	16 31	10 44	9 21	22 26	7 26	16 01

Day	Sidereal Time	☽ Node					DECLINATIONS					
	H M S		☉	☽	☿	♀	♂	♃	♄	♅	♆	♇
1	16:41:39	27♊58	21S51	21N55	22S08	19S07	14S36	22N36	20N19	15S04	18S32	12S52
3	16:49:32	27 52	22 09	24 13	22 49	19 43	14 04	22 38	20 18	15 03	18 31	12 52
5	16:57:25	27 46	22 25	26 20	23 20	17 13	13 32	22 39	20 17	15 02	18 30	12 53
7	17:05:19	27 39	22 39	12 05	23 58	20 48	12 59	22 41	20 16	15 01	18 30	12 53
9	17:13:12	27 33	22 51	1 00	24 25	21 17	12 25	22 42	20 16	14 59	18 29	12 54
11	17:21:05	27 26	23 01	10S11	24 47	21 44	11 52	22 44	20 14	14 58	18 28	12 54
13	17:28:58	27 20	23 10	19 06	25 04	22 08	11 18	22 45	20 13	14 57	18 27	12 55
15	17:36:51	27 14	23 17	23 22	25 15	22 29	10 43	22 47	20 11	14 56	18 26	12 56
17	17:44:44	27 07	23 22	23 24	25 21	23 04	10 09	22 49	20 10	14 54	18 25	12 57
19	17:52:37	27 01	23 25	18 34	25 21	23 04	9 34	22 50	20 09	14 53	18 25	12 57
21	18:00:30	26 55	23 26	10 45	25 15	23 17	8 58	22 52	20 08	14 51	18 24	12 58
23	18:08:23	26 48	23 26	1 22	25 02	23 28	8 23	22 54	20 07	14 49	18 23	12 58
25	18:16:17	26 42	23 23	8N28	24 44	23 35	7 47	22 55	20 07	14 47	18 22	12 58
27	18:24:10	26 36	23 19	17 22	24 20	23 39	7 11	22 57	20 06	14 46	18 21	12 59
29	18:32:03	26 29	23 12	23 13	23 49	23 41	6 35	22 59	20 05	14 44	18 20	13 00
31	18:39:56	26 23	23 04	23 40	23 13	23 40	5 59	23 00	20 04	14 42	18 19	13 00

57

2001 ASTEROIDS									
	CERES ⚳		PALLAS ⚴		JUNO ⚵		VESTA ⚶		CHIRON ⚷
	LONG.	DECL.	LONG.	DECL.	LONG.	DECL.	LONG.	DECL.	LONG.	DECL.
Jan 1	16✗41	21S03	22♏49	1N51	6♓21	10S33	26≈36	17S19	22✗36	18S15
5	18 18	21 18	24 22	2 05	8 09	10 05	28 26	16 40	23 03	18 15
9	19 55	21 32	25 53	2 21	9 59	9 35	0♓17	16 00	23 29	18 15
13	21 31	21 45	27 23	2 40	11 51	9 04	2 08	15 20	23 54	18 15
17	23 05	21 57	28 51	3 01	13 45	8 32	4 00	14 39	24 19	18 14
21	24 39	22 08	0♑16	3 25	15 40	7 58	5 53	13 57	24 44	18 14
25	26 12	22 18	1 40	3 50	17 38	7 22	7 46	13 14	25 07	18 13
29	27 43	22 27	3 01	4 19	19 37	6 46	9 39	12 31	25 30	18 12
Feb 2	29 13	22 36	4 19	4 49	21 38	6 09	11 33	11 48	25 52	18 11
6	0♑41	22 42	5 35	5 22	23 41	-5 30	13 27	11 04	26 13	18 09
10	2 08	22 48	6 48	5 57	25 45	4 51	15 21	10 20	26 33	18 08
14	3 33	22 53	7 57	6 35	27 50	4 11	17 16	9 35	26 51	18 06
18	4 57	22 58	9 03	7 15	29 57	3 30	19 10	8 50	27 09	18 04
22	6 19	23 02	10 06	7 57	2♈05	2 49	21 05	8 05	27 25	18 02
26	7 38	23 06	11 04	8 42	4 14	2 07	22 59	7 20	27 41	18 00
Mar 2	8 56	23 09	11 58	9 28	6 24	1 25	24 54	6 35	27 55	17 58
6	10 11	23 12	12 48	10 16	8 36	0 43	26 48	5 50	28 07	17 56
10	11 23	23 15	13 32	11 06	10 48	0 00	28 43	5 05	28 18	17 53
14	12 34	23 18	14 12	11 58	13 01	0N42	0♉37	4 20	28 28	17 51
18	13 41	23 20	14 46	12 51	15 16	1 25	2 31	3 35	28 36	17 48
22	14 43	23 23	15 14	13 45	17 31	2 07	4 25	2 50	28 43	17 46
26	15 47	23 26	15 35	14 40	19 47	2 49	6 18	2 06	28 49	17 43
30	16 45	23 29	15 50	15 36	22 03	3 31	8 11	1 22	28 53	17 40
April 3	17 39	23 32	15 59	16 32	24 21	4 13	10 04	0 39	28 55	17 38
7	18 30	23 36	16R00	17 28	26 39	4 53	11 57	0N04	28R56	17 35
11	19 17	23 41	15 53	18 23	28 58	5 33	13 49	0 46	28 55	17 32
15	20 00	23 46	15 39	19 18	1♉17	6 13	15 40	1 28	28 53	17 30
19	20 39	23 53	15 18	20 11	3 37	6 51	17 32	2 10	28 49	17 27
23	21 13	24 00	14 48	21 03	5 57	7 29	19 22	2 50	28 44	17 24
27	21 42	24 08	14 11	21 52	8 18	8 05	21 12	3 30	28 38	17 22
May 1	22 06	24 18	13 27	22 38	10 39	8 40	23 02	4 09	28 30	17 20
5	22 25	24 29	12 36	23 21	13 00	9 14	24 51	4 47	28 21	17 17
9	22 39	24 41	11 39	24 00	15 22	9 47	26 39	5 25	28 11	17 15
13	22 47	24 55	10 37	24 36	17 44	10 18	28 26	6 01	28 00	17 13
17	22R49	25 10	9 31	25 06	20 06	10 47	0♊13	6 37	27 47	17 11
21	22 45	25 26	8 21	25 32	22 28	11 15	1 59	7 11	27 34	17 09
25	22 35	25 43	7 10	25 53	24 50	11 42	3 44	7 45	27 20	17 07
29	22 20	26 02	5 58	26 08	27 13	12 06	5 28	8 17	27 06	17 05
Jun 2	21 59	26 22	4 47	26 18	29 35	12 28	7 11	8 49	26 50	17 03
6	21 32	26 43	3 38	26 22	1♊58	12 49	8 53	9 19	26 35	17 02
10	21 00	27 04	2 32	26 22	4 20	13 08	10 34	9 48	26 19	17 01
14	20 23	27 26	1 31	26 16	6 42	13 24	12 14	10 16	26 02	16 60
18	19 42	27 48	0 35	26 05	9 04	13 39	13 53	10 43	25 46	16 59
22	18 56	28 10	29♏46	25 49	11 26	13 51	15 30	11 09	25 30	16 58
26	18 08	28 32	29 02	25 29	13 47	14 01	17 06	11 33	25 14	16 57
30	17 17	28 52	28 28	25 05	16 08	14 09	18 41	11 56	24 58	16 57

Noon Greenwich Mean Time

	CERES ⚳		PALLAS ⚴		JUNO ⚵		VESTA ⚶		CHIRON ⚷	
	LONG.	DECL.	LONG.	DECL.	LONG.	DECL.	LONG.	DECL.	LONG.	DECL.
July 4	16R25	29S12	27R58	24N37	18♊29	14N15	20♉04	12N18	24R43	16S56
8	15♋32	29 31	27♏36	24 06	20 49	14 19	21 46	12 39	24♐28	16 56
12	14 40	29 48	27 22	23 32	23 08	14 20	23 16	12 58	24 14	16 56
16	13 48	30 03	27 15	22 56	25 27	14 20	24 44	13 16	24 01	16 56
20	12 59	30 17	27D15	22 17	27 46	14 17	26 11	13 33	23 49	16 56
24	12 12	30 29	27 22	21 36	0♋03	14 12	27 35	13 48	23 38	16 57
28	11 29	30 39	27 35	20 54	2 20	14 05	28 57	14 02	23 27	16 58
Aug 1	10 50	30 47	27 54	20 11	4 36	13 55	0♊16	14 15	23 18	16 59
5	10 16	30 54	28 19	19 27	6 51	13 44	1 34	14 26	23 11	16 60
9	9 47	30 59	28 50	18 42	9 05	13 31	2 48	14 37	23 04	17 01
13	9 23	31 03	29 25	17 57	11 18	13 16	4 00	14 46	22 59	17 02
17	9 05	31 05	0♐06	17 12	13 29	12 59	5 09	14 54	22 55	17 03
21	8 53	31 07	0 50	16 27	15 40	12 41	6 14	15 00	22 53	17 05
25	8 46	31 07	1 39	15 42	17 49	12 22	7 16	15 06	22 52	17 07
29	8D46	31 06	2 32	14 58	19 57	11 59	8 14	15 10	22D52	17 08
Sep 2	8 51	31 04	3 28	14 14	22 03	11 35	9 09	15 13	22 54	17 10
6	9 01	31 02	4 28	13 30	24 08	11 11	9 59	15 16	22 57	17 12
10	9 17	30 59	5 31	12 48	26 11	10 45	10 44	15 17	23 02	17 14
14	9 38	30 55	6 36	12 07	28 12	10 18	11 25	15 17	23 08	17 16
18	10 04	30 51	7 45	11 26	0♋11	9 50	12 00	15 17	23 16	17 18
22	10 34	30 46	8 55	10 47	2 08	9 21	12 30	15 15	23 24	17 21
26	11 09	30 40	10 08	10 09	4 03	8 51	12 54	15 13	23 35	17 23
30	11 49	30 34	11 24	9 32	5 56	8 20	13 12	15 10	23 46	17 25
Oct 4	12 32	30 27	12 41	8 56	7 46	7 49	13 24	15 07	23 59	17 27
8	13 20	30 20	13 59	8 22	9 33	7 18	13 29	15 03	24 13	17 29
12	14 11	30 11	15 20	7 49	11 18	6 46	13R27	14 59	24 28	17 31
16	15 05	30 03	16 42	7 18	13 00	6 14	13 18	14 54	24 44	17 33
20	16 03	29 53	18 05	6 48	14 38	5 43	13 02	14 49	25 02	17 35
24	17 03	29 43	19 30	6 20	16 13	5 11	12 39	14 44	25 20	17 37
28	18 07	29 32	20 56	5 53	17 45	4 40	12 09	14 39	25 40	17 39
Nov 1	19 13	29 20	22 23	5 28	19 12	4 09	11 32	14 33	26 00	17 41
5	20 22	29 08	23 50	5 05	20 36	3 39	10 49	14 28	26 21	17 42
9	21 33	28 54	25 19	4 43	21 55	3 10	10 00	14 23	26 43	17 44
13	22 46	28 40	26 49	4 23	23 09	2 42	9 06	14 19	27 05	17 45
17	24 01	28 25	28 19	4 05	24 19	2 15	8 09	14 15	27 29	17 46
21	25 18	28 09	29 50	3 48	25 23	1 50	7 08	14 11	27 52	17 47
25	26 37	27 53	1♑21	3 33	26 21	1 26	6 05	14 08	28 17	17 48
29	27 57	27 35	2 53	3 20	27 13	1 04	5 02	14 06	28 42	17 49
Dec 3	29 19	27 17	4 25	3 09	27 59	0 45	4 00	14 05	29 07	17 49
7	0♒43	26 57	5 57	2 59	28 38	0 28	2 59	14 05	29 32	17 49
11	2 07	26 37	7 29	2 51	29 11	0 13	2 02	14 07	29 58	17 49
15	3 33	26 16	9 02	2 45	29 35	0 02	1 09	14 10	0♓24	17 49
19	5 00	25 54	10 35	2 40	29 52	0S06	0 21	14 13	0 50	17 49
23	6 28	25 31	12 08	2 37	0♍01	0 11	29♉38	14 19	1 16	17 48
27	7 57	25 08	13 40	2 35	0R02	0 12	29 02	14 27	1 42	17 48
31	9 27	24 44	15 13	2 36	29♌55	0 09	28 33	14 35	2 07	17 47

Eclipses 2001

I. Total Eclipse of the Moon, January 9, 19♋39. The beginning of the umbral phase is visible in the northern region of Canada, most of Alaska, Greenland, Arctic, Europe, most of Africa, Australia, western Micronesia, Asia, Queen Mary coast of Antarctica, northeastern North Atlantic Ocean, east South Atlantic Ocean, Indian Ocean, and west North Pacific Ocean. The end is visible in northeast North America, Greenland, Arctic, northeast South America, Europe, Africa, Antarctica coast near Cape Ann, Asia, Atlantic Ocean, Indian Ocean, and western Philippine Sea.

Moon enters penumbra	17:43.5 GMT
Moon enters umbra	18:42.0 GMT
Moon enters totality	19:49.5 GMT
Middle of eclipse	20:20.5 GMT
Moon leaves totality	20:51.6 GMT
Moon leaves umbra	21:59.1 GMT
Moon leaves penumbra	22:57.6 GMT

II. Total Eclipse of the Sun, June 21, 0♋10. Visible in the South Atlantic, Angola, Zambia, Zimbabwe, Mozambique, Madagascar, and Indian Ocean.

Eclipse begins	9:32.9 GMT
Beginning of northern limit of umbra	10:36.5 GMT
Beginning of center line; central eclipse begins	10:37.0 GMT
Beginning of southern limit of umbra	10:37.6 GMT
Central eclipse at local apparent noon	11:57.8 GMT
End of southern limit of umbra	13:29.8 GMT
End of center line; central eclipse ends	13:30.3 GMT
End of northern limit of umbra	13:30.8 GMT
Eclipse ends	14:34.3 GMT

III. Partial Eclipse of the Moon, July 5, 13♑39. The beginning of umbral phase is visible in Antarctica, Australia, New Zealand, east Asia except far

---

Most Visible* Meteor Showers

August 12 ±2 days Perseids: at 50 meteors per hour

October 10   Draconids (meteors per hour varies)

October 21 ±3 days Orionids: at 30 meteors per hour

November 17 ±3 days Leonids: at 10 meteors/hour

December 13 ±2 days Geminids: at 50 meteors/hour

* "Most Visible" refers to those occurring within 6 days of the New Moon.

north, Aleutians, Pacific Ocean except extreme east, and eastern Indian Ocean. The end is visible in Australia, Antarctica, New Zealand, Asia except extreme north, east Africa, west Pacific Ocean, and Indian Ocean.

Moon enters penumbra . . . . 12:10.8 GMT
Moon enters umbra . . . . 13:35.1 GMT
Middle of eclipse . . . . 14:55.2 GMT
Moon leaves umbra . . . . 16:15.3 GMT
Moon leaves penumbra . . . . 17:39.7 GMT

IV. Annular Eclipse of the Sun, December 14, 22♐56. An annular eclipse is where a narrow ring of the Sun is visible beyond the dark mask of the moon. This eclipse is visible in the Pacific Ocean, northwestern South America, Central America, the U.S., and western and southern Canada.

Eclipse begins . . . . 18:03.3 GMT
Beginning of southern limit of umbra . . . . 19:09.3 GMT
Beginning of center line; central eclipse begins . . . . 19:09.7 GMT
Beginning of northern limit of umbra . . . . 19:10.1 GMT
Central eclipse at local apparent noon . . . . 20:44.8 GMT
End of northern limit of umbra . . . . 22:33.8 GMT
End of center line; central eclipse ends . . . . 22:34.2 GMT
End of southern limit of umbra . . . . 22:34.5 GMT
Eclipse ends . . . . 23:40.6 GMT

V. Penumbral Eclipse of the Moon, December 30, 8♋48. Beginning of the penumbral phase is visible in North America, Central America, South America except east coast, Greenland, extreme northwest Europe, northeast Asia, Arctic, most of New Zealand, North Atlantic Ocean, Pacific Ocean, east Philippine Sea, and Coral Sea. The end is visible in North America except east coast, Greenland, Arctic, northern Central America, Asia, Indonesia, Australia, New Zealand, North Pacific Ocean, South Pacific Ocean except southeast, and eastern Indian Ocean.

Moon enters penumbra . . . . 8:25.4 GMT
Middle of eclipse . . . . 10:29.2 GMT
Moon leaves penumbra . . . . 12:33.2 GMT

Table of Ascendants at 40° North Latitude

Date	Hour of the Day, Local Mean Time											
	0	2	4	6	8	10	12	14	16	18	20	22
Jan. 1	8♎	2♏	26♏	21♐	19♑	29♒	19♈	1♊	2♋	27♋	21♌	15♍
Jan. 11	16♎	10♏	4♐	29♐	1♒	14♓	4♉	13♊	11♋	5♌	29♌	23♍
Jan. 21	24♎	18♏	12♐	9♑	13♒	1♈	18♉	23♊	19♋	13♌	7♍	1♎
Jan. 31	2♏	26♏	20♐	19♑	28♒	18♈	1♊	2♋	27♋	21♌	15♍	9♎
Feb. 10	10♏	3♐	29♐	0♒	14♓	3♉	12♊	11♋	5♌	29♌	23♍	17♎
Feb. 20	17♏	11♐	8♑	13♒	0♈	18♉	22♊	19♋	13♌	7♍	1♎	24♎
Mar. 2	25♏	20♐	18♑	27♒	17♈	1♊	1♋	27♋	21♌	14♍	8♎	2♏
Mar. 12	3♐	28♐	29♑	13♓	3♉	11♊	10♋	5♌	28♌	22♍	16♎	10♏
Mar. 22	11♐	8♑	12♒	29♓	17♉	22♊	18♋	12♌	6♍	0♎	24♎	18♏
Apr. 1	19♐	18♑	26♒	16♈	0♊	1♋	26♋	20♌	14♍	8♎	2♏	26♏
Apr. 11	28♐	29♑	11♓	0♉	11♊	10♋	4♌	28♌	22♍	16♎	10♏	3♐
Apr. 21	7♑	11♒	28♓	16♉	21♊	18♋	12♌	6♍	0♎	24♎	17♏	11♐
May 1	17♑	25♒	15♈	29♉	0♋	26♋	20♌	14♍	8♎	1♏	25♏	20♐
May 11	28♑	11♓	1♉	10♊	9♋	4♌	28♌	21♍	15♎	9♏	3♐	28♐
May 21	11♒	28♓	16♉	21♊	18♋	12♌	5♍	29♍	23♎	17♏	11♐	8♑
May 31	25♒	14♈	28♉	0♋	25♋	19♌	13♍	7♎	1♏	25♏	19♐	18♑
Jun. 10	10♓	0♉	10♊	9♋	3♌	27♌	21♍	15♎	9♏	3♐	28♐	29♑
Jun. 20	27♓	15♉	20♊	17♋	11♌	5♍	29♍	23♎	17♏	11♐	7♑	11♒
Jun. 30	14♈	28♉	29♊	25♋	19♌	13♍	7♎	1♏	24♏	19♐	17♑	25♒
July 10	0♉	9♊	8♋	3♌	27♌	21♍	15♎	8♏	2♐	27♐	28♑	11♓
July 20	14♉	20♊	17♋	11♌	5♍	29♍	22♎	16♏	10♐	7♑	11♒	28♓
July 30	27♉	29♊	25♋	19♌	12♍	6♎	0♏	24♏	18♐	17♑	25♒	14♈
Aug. 9	9♊	8♋	3♌	26♌	20♍	14♎	8♏	2♐	27♐	28♑	10♓	0♉
Aug. 19	19♊	16♋	10♌	4♍	28♍	22♎	16♏	10♐	6♑	10♒	27♓	15♉
Aug. 29	29♊	24♋	18♌	12♍	6♎	0♏	24♏	18♐	16♑	24♒	13♈	28♉
Sep. 8	7♋	2♌	26♌	20♍	14♎	8♏	1♐	27♐	27♑	9♓	29♈	9♊
Sep. 18	16♋	10♌	4♍	28♍	22♎	15♏	9♐	6♑	9♒	26♓	14♉	20♊
Sep. 28	24♋	18♌	12♍	6♎	29♎	23♏	18♐	16♑	23♒	13♈	27♉	29♊
Oct. 8	2♌	26♌	19♍	13♎	7♏	1♐	26♐	26♑	8♓	29♈	9♊	8♋
Oct. 18	10♌	3♍	27♍	21♎	15♏	9♐	6♑	10♒	25♓	13♉	18♊	16♋
Oct. 28	17♌	11♍	5♎	29♎	23♏	17♐	16♑	24♒	12♈	26♉	27♊	24♋
Nov. 7	25♌	19♍	13♎	7♏	1♐	26♐	26♑	8♓	28♈	8♊	7♋	2♌
Nov. 17	3♍	27♍	21♎	15♏	8♐	5♑	8♒	24♓	13♉	18♊	16♋	10♌
Nov. 27	11♍	5♎	29♎	22♏	17♐	14♑	22♒	11♈	26♉	28♊	24♋	18♌
Dec. 7	19♍	13♎	6♏	0♐	25♐	25♑	7♓	27♈	7♊	7♋	2♌	25♌
Dec. 17	26♍	20♎	14♏	8♐	4♑	7♒	23♓	12♉	18♊	15♋	10♌	3♍
Dec. 27	4♎	28♎	22♏	16♐	14♑	21♒	10♈	25♉	28♊	23♋	17♌	11♍

	Sunrise Northern Latitudes						Sunset Northern Latitudes					
Date	10°	20°	30°	40°	50°	60°	10°	20°	30°	40°	50°	60°
Jan. 5	6:19	6:36	6:57	7:22	7:58	8:59	5:53	5:35	5:15	4:49	4:14	3:12
15	6:21	6:38	6:57	7:20	7:52	8:47	5:58	5:41	5:23	5:00	4:27	3:33
25	6:23	6:37	6:54	7:14	7:42	8:29	6:02	5:48	5:31	5:11	4:43	3:57
Feb. 4	6:22	6:34	6:48	7:05	7:29	8:06	6:06	5:54	5:40	5:23	5:00	4:23
14	6:20	6:30	6:40	6:54	7:12	7:40	6:09	5:59	5:48	5:35	5:17	4:50
24	6:16	6:23	6:31	6:40	6:53	7:12	6:10	6:03	5:56	5:47	5:34	5:15
Mar. 6	6:12	6:16	6:20	6:25	6:32	6:43	6:11	6:07	6:03	5:58	5:51	5:41
16	6:06	6:07	6:08	6:09	6:11	6:13	6:11	6:10	6:09	6:08	6:07	6:06
26	6:01	5:59	5:56	5:53	5:49	5:43	6:11	6:13	6:15	6:18	6:23	6:30
April 5	5:55	5:50	5:44	5:37	5:28	5:12	6:10	6:15	6:21	6:29	6:39	6:54
15	5:49	5:42	5:33	5:22	5:07	4:43	6:10	6:18	6:27	6:39	6:54	7:19
25	5:45	5:34	5:23	5:08	4:47	4:14	6:11	6:22	6:34	6:49	7:10	7:44
May 5	5:41	5:28	5:14	4:55	4:29	3:46	6:12	6:25	6:40	6:59	7:25	8:09
15	5:39	5:24	5:06	4:45	4:14	3:22	6:14	6:29	6:47	7:09	7:40	8:33
25	5:38	5:21	5:01	4:37	4:02	3:01	6:16	6:33	6:53	7:18	7:53	8:55
June 4	5:38	5:20	4:59	4:32	3:54	2:45	6:19	6:37	6:58	7:25	8:03	9:13
14	5:39	5:20	4:58	4:31	3:50	2:36	6:21	6:40	7:02	7:30	8:11	9:25
24	5:41	5:22	5:00	4:32	3:52	2:37	6:24	6:43	7:05	7:33	8:13	9:28
July 4	5:44	5:25	5:04	4:37	3:57	2:46	6:25	6:44	7:05	7:32	8:11	9:22
14	5:46	5:29	5:09	4:43	4:07	3:02	6:25	6:43	7:03	7:28	8:04	9:08
24	5:48	5:33	5:14	4:51	4:19	3:23	6:25	6:40	6:58	7:21	7:53	8:48
Aug. 3	5:50	5:36	5:20	5:00	4:33	3:46	6:22	6:36	6:51	7:11	7:39	8:24
13	5:51	5:39	5:26	5:10	4:47	4:10	6:19	6:30	6:43	6:59	7:21	7:58
23	5:51	5:42	5:32	5:19	5:02	4:34	6:14	6:22	6:32	6:45	7:02	7:29
Sept. 2	5:51	5:45	5:38	5:29	5:17	4:58	6:08	6:14	6:21	6:29	6:41	6:59
12	5:50	5:47	5:43	5:38	5:32	5:22	6:02	6:05	6:09	6:13	6:19	6:29
22	5:49	5:49	5:48	5:48	5:47	5:45	5:56	5:56	5:56	5:57	5:57	5:59
Oct. 2	5:49	5:51	5:54	5:58	6:02	6:09	5:50	5:47	5:44	5:40	5:36	5:29
12	5:48	5:54	6:00	6:08	6:18	6:33	5:44	5:39	5:32	5:25	5:14	4:59
22	5:49	5:57	6:07	6:18	6:34	6:58	5:40	5:31	5:22	5:10	4:54	4:30
Nov. 1	5:51	6:02	6:14	6:29	6:50	7:23	5:36	5:25	5:13	4:57	4:36	4:03
11	5:53	6:07	6:22	6:41	7:07	7:49	5:35	5:21	5:06	4:47	4:21	3:39
21	5:57	6:13	6:30	6:52	7:23	8:14	5:35	5:19	5:01	4:39	4:09	3:18
Dec. 1	6:02	6:19	6:38	7:03	7:37	8:36	5:37	5:19	5:00	4:35	4:01	3:02
11	6:07	6:25	6:46	7:12	7:49	8:53	5:40	5:22	5:01	4:35	3:58	2:54
21	6:12	6:31	6:52	7:18	7:56	9:02	5:45	5:26	5:05	4:38	4:01	2:54
31	6:16	6:35	6:56	7:22	7:59	9:03	5:49	5:32	5:11	4:45	4:08	3:04

Sunrise times are AM, sunset times are PM, Local Mean Time. **Local Mean Time** is converted to Standard Time by adding four minutes for each degree of longitude a locality is west of that Time Zone's standard meridian (75° EST, 90° CST, 105° MST, 120° PST, etc.) *or* by subtracting four minutes for each degree east of the standard meridian. If **Daylight Saving Time** is being used, **add one hour.**

More Calendars and Books

Pocket Astrologer® is also available as a full color, 40-page wall calendar, **Celestial Influences**,® which unfolds to 12 x 18 inches. A third format is the **Celestial Guide**,® a week-at-a-glance engagement calendar with either a wire-O binding or as loose, unbound, 3-hole punched pages which include an ephemeris and address book (176 pages, 5½ x 8½ inches, illustrated).

Celestial Influences® 2001 wall calendar $9.95

Pocket Astrologer® 2001 .... $4.95

Celestial Guide® 2001 engagement calendar, wire bound edition $9.95

Celestial Guide® 2001 loose pages, 3-hole punched edition $9.95
Prices effective through August 2001.

The Little Giant Encyclopedia of the Zodiac. A complete, straightforward resource of Chinese and Western astrology. A must-have for entertainment or as a tool for living harmoniously with one's natural character. 510 pages, 4³⁄₁₆ x 5⁵⁄₁₆ inches, paperback $9.95

Putting it Up with Honey: A Natural Foods Canning and Preserving Cookbook, by Susan Geiskopf. "Putting food by" with honey! Over 200 tasty and nutritious recipes for preserving food without sugar or harmful preservatives. 224 pages, 8 x 8 inches, illustrated, indexed $11.95

Fast & Natural Cuisine: A Complete Guide to Vegetarian and Seafood Cooking, by Susann Geiskopf and Mindy Toomay. Delicious and delightful natural food meals in 25 to 45 minutes for people on the go! 256 pages, 8 x 8 inches, illustrated, indexed $12.95

To order: Send check or money order, including shipping and handling, to Quicksilver Productions or send information for Visa or MasterCard.

Shipping & Handling: Include $3⁰⁰ per order for Bookrate-Insured shipping (add $2⁵⁰ each additional shipment to others). Subtract $1⁰⁰ if payment is made by check, cash, or money order. FedEx-Ground shipping is $6⁰⁰, less $1⁰⁰ for payment by check, cash, or money order and you must include a weekday street address.

For Air Mail or foreign orders, please write, fax, or email for information.

Discounts: Subtract either 10% for orders over $50 or 15% if over $100.

Send orders to: **Quicksilver Productions, Dept. PAK2**
P.O. Box 340, Ashland, Oregon 97520 U.S.A.
Voice: (541) 482-5343   FAX: (541) 482-0960
celestialcalendars@email.com